CW00550294

Shamanic Engineering

Spiritual and shamanic based exercises for empowerment, connection and charting a new course in life.

Trevor Cowan

Self Published

Shamanic Engineering

Spiritual and shamanic based exercises for empowerment, connection and charting a new course in life.

Copyright © 2022 by Trevor Cowan

email: Trevor@ShamanicHelp.org
website: ShamanicHelp.org

All rights reserved. No part of this publication may be reproduced, stored in a retrieval system, or transmitted, in any form or by any means (electronic, mechanical, photocopying, recording or otherwise), without the prior written permission of the publisher, except by reviewers, who may quote brief passages in a review.

This publication is sold under the express understanding that any decisions or actions you take as a result of reading this book must be based on your judgement and will be at your sole risk. The author will not be held responsible for the consequences of any actions and/or decisions taken as a result of any information given or recommendations made.

This book is not intended as a substitute for the medical advice of physicians. The reader should regularly consult a physician in matters relating to his/her health and particularly with respect to any symptoms that may require diagnosis or medical attention.

The views and opinions expressed in this book are solely that of the author.

ISBN 978-1-7397019-0-1

1st edition published 2022 by Trevor Cowan.

cover photograph from shutterstock.com
back photographs © Trevor Cowan

For dad. The bravest man I know.

Contents

Preface

It is my hope in writing this book to show that we are intrinsically a part of the natural world, linked throughout time by our ancestral lineage and the energies that pervade the planet. Those that have lived in connection with all that is had a wisdom of their own, one that it still pertinent today and helpful to anyone on their life journey, be they spiritual or not. With the compendium of exercises and ideas presented I am sharing some of the ancient wisdom that I have been privileged to have been taught, along with my own commentary around philosophy, psychology and how science and spirituality are entwined, with the boundaries often blurred. My rational and logical engineering background has afforded me the ability to look at some of the spiritual concepts presented from a different perspective, and I hope sheds a light on what some would call the mystical or esoteric.

In my own shamanic healing work I engineer solutions to problems, using some of the tools and techniques outlined in this book, and hope that you will be able to make use of them to help engineer solutions and possibilities for yourself, showing that you can make great strides spiritually and emotionally without the need to defer to others, or be reliant on other people for guidance. However ordinary, normal, unremarkable, without training or uneducated in spiritual matters you may think you are, you have the ability to change and heal yourself. You can work on yourself, illuminate your gifts and rediscover a more purposeful life as you strengthen your connection to the natural world and your life path, and in doing so become a more authentic version of you. Everyone has a right to their own beliefs. So there should be eight billion religions on this planet, eight billion spiritual beliefs. Reading through and working with some of the exercises in this book will hopefully unearth a clearer idea of what yours are.

This book has been written as a guide, a work book of self discovery to some degree, with tools and techniques to help you on your spiritual journey by working towards clearing any emotional or psychological blocks, re-connecting to the natural world and better understanding your place within it. Although this is an introduction to contemporary shamanism, and draws upon earth connected wisdom, this is not a teach yourself shamanism book. The best way to learn about this ancient practice is from direct teaching, as it is the shamanic teacher's experience and lineage that is the gateway for authentic understanding.

Shamanism has become popular in recent years, but in its contemporary form differs from that practised by indigenous nature connected cultures, so as to be useful in the current more urbanised environments. My use of the word shamanism can loosely be interpreted to mean nature based spirituality that encompasses teachings and wisdom past down the generations, mixed with practices adapted for the modern world.

There are many contemporary shamanic practitioners around the globe offering healings and, if qualified, teaching shamanism in a modern way, sharing their knowledge with those willing to learn. But there are also many opportunities and activities available to the layperson that can open one up to the world of community, magic and ceremony, such as meditation groups, drumming circles, spiritual retreats and mind, body and soul festivals, not to mention the wide range of online resources concerning shamanism and spirituality in general.

I have written this book based on my own experiences, my own spiritual journey and the teachings passed on to me, with the underlying intention being to share what I have learnt to help others in an accessible and practical way. In my opinion, if something is useful, then I believe others have a right to know about it, so it may help them with their own journey. The time of keeping things hidden is not what is needed in today's society. The maxim 'knowledge is power' certainly holds a truth but I believe sharing knowledge is what is necessary in the current world, sharing this power with all people. Additionally, why can't anyone find their own path and why wouldn't some of the tools and techniques be common across all peoples? If they work, they work. If you were born into a Christian family does that preclude you from deciding your own path and embracing lets say Tibetan shamanism, Hinduism, Judaism, or pagan witchcraft? Why can't you choose your own path and take with you that which is helpful from your own culture and mix it with the new. New Age doesn't mean diluted, it means bringing together, refining and adapting. Of course many honour their ancestors by keeping their traditions alive and as authentic as possible, but for those who do not have an obvious lineage to such practices, we have to adopt, adapt and even create our own. New traditions, adapted from the old are what are required in the modern world. Prayers for rain to water crops, protection for the warriors who are going to battle with the neighbouring tribe, or offerings to the ocean spirits for calm seas for fishing, have little resonance in the world today, where we live in urbanised areas, next to thousands, sometimes millions of others, with our connection to the planet through a gadget in our hands, and where the day to day pressures are around money, security, relationships and the use of time.

Any tools that can be useful in the modern world should be shared wherever they are from, whoever developed them. Modern shamanism is flexible, not rigid, not fear based. The ancestors, those that have gone before, would only want the people of this planet to grow. They would only want more love to be spread, not negativity, anger, resentment or rigidity. Wouldn't a wise elder, a beloved ancestor, guru, mystic, shaman, deity, goddess or god say "Share the love, don't keep it for yourself".

Everyone has a right to know about the ancient knowledge and wisdom at the core of shamanism and nature based spirituality, used for millennia to help people around the globe. That said, I have endeavoured not to reveal any of the practices that should only be passed on through direct teaching, including some that could be thought of as more sacred or powerful, as they do not translate easily into word form and require the guidance of a qualified shamanic practitioner to be taught effectively. Also, as the exercises described in this book are wide ranging and drawn from many different areas, it is likely there are similarities with more traditional processes, even those conducted within a religious framework, but the similarity is purely coincidental and not meant to be copying, appropriating or disrespectful.

This book contains practical and written exercises, along with some ideas and concepts to help you familiarise yourself with spirituality and the ancient methodology of shamanism, to understand your own life and see your place in the world from a perspective that you may not have come across before.

Please note, the written exercises are suggested for those people that are drawn to writing. For many, writing does not comes naturally so as an alternative either record your answers and insights on your phone, or simply think and contemplate upon each exercise or issue described, maybe finding an object in nature that can represent it and can act as a reminder for you do any *deeper* work later. Shamanism has, after all, been effective for thousands of years without the written word.

Goal

Your soul can be thought of as a beautiful gem hidden within you, metaphorically buried in the earth that is you. It has always been there, waiting for you to unearth it, to reconnect to it. Maybe it has been buried deeply, covered in soil, sand and stone. Buried so far down into the earth that it needs dynamite to blast away the rock, then a mechanical excavator to remove the next few layers, before finally digging with a shovel, or hand tool, to unearth it. For some this precious gem may be near the surface and easily dug out with a trowel, but then it still requires cleaning with a brush to start to see its radiance. For those that have the gem already in their possession, a final buffing or polish with the softest of cloths will make it sparkle like no other jewel and become the beacon it was meant to be.

The engineer in me likes this analogy, marrying the ethereal soul to the search for, mining of and final polishing of a gemstone. Engineering meets spirituality, and the process of choosing the right tools for the job. You don't use a sledgehammer to crack a nut as they say. So the exercises included in this book vary in their strength or potency; some being explosive, bringing instantaneous results and insight, others more subtle and perhaps more applicable to the polishing stage. It is up to you to decide which are which, and this will only become apparent when you try them. If some exercises seem pointless or do not resonate, then that is fine, please move on and leave them until they do seem appropriate. It is, of course, a waste of time trying to dig down fifty metres with a teaspoon.

Introduction

"You have to let it all go Neo. Fear, doubt, disbelief.
Free your mind."
Morpheus, The Matrix.

What shapes us? What moulds us into the person we are? For a start there is information. The information we have inherited, been taught and discovered for ourselves. Access to information is at an all time high. You can search for information on any subject under the sun (or beyond the sun for that matter). But where amongst this information overload is knowledge, truth and wisdom? What filters has this information gone through? Has it been manipulated? How do you know?

It begins with trust. In fact, life begins with trust. A newborn is totally at the mercy of the world and it is the role and responsibility of the parents or guardians to look after that infant. The child trusts the parents implicitly. As the child grows this trust is often extended to all the people the child meets, where the feeling received (or perceived) from the parents, is that this new person is friend not foe. So a child naturally trusts and learns to defer to an adult, accepting innocently what the adult says and does.

Arguably the biggest factor influencing the child, is the environment it grows up in, from the immediate geography and climate of the area it has been born into, along with the local and national cultural influences, to specifically the child's family and their social and economic level. As Aristotle, the great Greek philosopher said *"Give me a child until he is seven and I will show you the man."*

Parents want what is best for their children, to keep them safe and, understandably, wish to give them more than they had when they were young, specifically when it comes to opportunities in life. But how much of what they were taught do they pass on to their children? Probably quite a lot, which again, is only natural. This is a founding principle of life and, at the most basic level, animal survival. Parents pass on what they have been taught to their offspring. Some common expressions, popular in England, relating to the natural inheritance of characteristics include "If it was good enough for me, then it's good enough for you", said by a parent to a child, and "Like father, like son", or "You sound just like your mother". No doubt, we have all picked up on such expressions when we were young and now, in adulthood, regurgitate them to our own children, if we have them, as a form of perceived wisdom.

Unfortunately not only is the good passed on, but also the not so good. From the seemingly innocuous finger wagging, high expectation goal setting and the unconscious sharing of bad habits, to being ignored, neglected, or even abandoned, not to mention the potentially life shattering verbal abusing, beating, or molestation of a child. Our worlds as children are shaped by the influencers in our lives and we trust adults to teach us the right way to live. As children we naturally adopt parental mannerisms, characteristics and quite often their religious or spiritual beliefs. There is no choice as a child.

The home life you are brought up within defines what is the norm for you. How often has it been said by a child that they thought this was normal, especially when referring to some negative behaviour or lifestyle when growing up. If you had to walk an hour to school, you would think this normal. If you went to church every Sunday you believed this to be normal. If you got whipped with your father's belt when you did something wrong then you would grow up to think this too was how all children were raised. And sadly, in this last case, as an adult the patterns of behaviour may continue, as parents often behave in a similar way with their own offspring.

At school, the child comes across new rules and systems as the educational establishments impose their own filters and biases, their institutional standards and their own take on the correct curriculum to teach the child. Modern schooling tries, I believe, in most countries to produce rounded, well educated, independent students. How successful it is at this is of course open to vast debate.

Also there is gender and the biases that boys and girls are treated with when growing up. Traditional gender stereotypes are often reinforced by parental, school and cultural behaviours. Gender fluidity is a relatively new concept but undoubtedly has always been there, even if swept under the carpet by parents or authority figures, out of fear, lack of understanding or prejudice. A boy raised to be a real man, to fight, to be strong, to not show emotion, will become a certain type of man. One raised with love, compassion, encouraged to share emotions, to be accepting and not be overly pressured will become another sort of man. Similarly for girls. Having to wear pretty pink outfits, given dolls to play with and helping mum with the cooking are memories that many British (and undoubtedly other nations) women probably have, reinforcing the female gender roles of having to look a certain way and learn about motherhood and housekeeping. There are biological differences, of course, and hormones and body chemistry to consider, but stereotype reinforcement and parenting styles have a major effect on a child's development.

So, in our western societies, children are products of their environments with very little space to explore what is beyond the influences described above and no way to gauge the extent of any dysfunctional upbringing. It is only later in life when the child, or more likely the young adult, starts to really question life for his or herself, that they look towards understanding their own identity and place in the world. However, does a teenager have the skill set necessary to make informed choices regarding all the information taught, shared, or sought out? Especially in the case of information from the internet, where a huge amount of filtration, bias and opinion can distort the facts.

We are the first generations with information at our fingertips (literally, in the form of smartphones), available almost constantly, wherever we are in the world via the web. This information overload has now been capitalised upon by corporations as they tailor feed, based on our internet click habits and viewing patterns, to give us more of what they think we want (predominately with the goal of making money, rather than any form of expansive education). Online we can discover people who think the same, look the same, and seemingly have similar ideas, desires and goals as ourselves. Our online tribe. Such copying behaviour is encouraged, even if what is found can be deemed as being at odds with living a happy and healthy life. For example, in the case of online influencers, teenage followers want to look like them, or follow their *beauty* advice (often sponsored by products they are paid to pedal), with unachievable expectations. For the more easily influenced individuals such unfulfilled expectations can lead to depression, or in the extreme cases, suicidal thoughts or actions.

As soon as we have an online presence, almost a given for any teenager or adolescent, we are open to have our seemingly innocuous posts, photos, and videos of friends, holidays or celebrations criticised by others, and possibly even open to abuse and threats. Such online trolling can only have a negative impact on the psyche, especially on that of the young, creating doubts and fears in areas of behaviour where such feelings are in no way justified.

But we want our children to experience freedom, not be worried or concerned about every action they take, online or in the real world. We want them to play and have fun, to mix with others, to learn, to grow. But of course, due to the negative experiences and potentially hazardous situations perceived, rules have been imposed for their safety. Rules around where to play, who to play with, what to eat, what to touch, who to talk to, etc. To always be safe; safe at school, safe online, safe crossing the road, safe mixing with others, safe at night and so on. We are removing children's ability to trust and have faith in themselves, by building this layer of protection around them; this shield of rules.

Children today are pushed to succeed from an early age, are exposed to many negative news stories, escape on their phones with music, social media and games, and have to deflect constant criticism on how they look and what they should think. All in all it seems pretty tough to be a child in the modern western world.

But is it any easier being an adult? Where does one find peace nowadays? Wherever you live you do not have to wait long before hearing the sound of construction, passing traffic (on the road and in the air), dogs barking, alarms, power tools, grass cutting, or music blaring out. The sounds of nature are being drowned out, or worse diminished, due to loss of habitat, destroyed by man's sprawl. Light pollution is flooding the night sky too and depriving us of one of the most incredible natural sights, the milky way streaking overhead. How many of the next generations will ever see it with their own eyes?

So much is changing, from the loss of clear skies and ancient forests, to the pollution of our lands, the seas and the air we breathe, even the extinction of whole species. It is terribly sad if one stops, steps back and looks at what has happened since the start of the industrial revolution, only two hundred years ago. Perhaps more so in the recent accelerated information age of the past twenty-five years. The pros of such progress have become almost a given; material goods, fast foods, a constant fuel and energy supply, access to technology that provides instantaneous information, entertainment and communication, and a general acceptance that more is better. Such pros seem to outweigh the cons, or at least disguise them to some degree.

This constant demand for more is very self centric, and as the haves parade themselves on social media, the have nots across the globe watch on their phones and decide they want this too, reinforcing the move to a global materialistic culture. Why can't the Bangladeshi woman want expensive shoes just like the woman in New York she sees on social media? She is not a better or worse person, but, of course, her circumstances and lifestyle are probably very different. Envy, jealousy and cultural differences can come into play and act as drivers of division, anger and hatred. This, however, is where the world has evolved to in recent times.

But let's return to trust. We all want to trust. As humans it is in our nature. We trust the Sun will come up in the morning. We trust the moon will change phase over the month. We trust the cycles of nature and the physical processes of our planet. But when it comes to the people we share the planet with where does our trust sit? Society forever increases it's list of rules to abide by and lawyers continue to leach off (sorry, of course I mean work to the letter of the law within) the system, which in turn demands we protect ourselves at every step in our affairs from litigation, and complete waivers, consent forms and sign various legal documents, that ultimately say we don't trust each other. A hand shake used to be all that was required, or a *gentlemen's agreement*, and I have no doubt that many still honour this. However, due to the power of governments and the laws created, a handshake has no legal standing, and must normally be backed up by a binding contract.

Although it happens in some areas, in general, the days of leaving your house unlocked are gone. In fact walls, fences, security cameras and alarms are on the increase. Lack of trust and the parallel increase in fear looks to be on the rise, let alone a loss of faith in politicians, governing bodies and others supposedly with our best interest at heart.

And do we trust ourselves? Shouldn't we at least trust our senses? For millennia they have kept us from eating poisonous or unhealthy foods, have told us if something is hot and will burn us, warned us of approaching danger, or alerted us to a far off call for help. What about our other perhaps less developed senses, such as gut instinct, intuition or any perceived spiritual guidance? Have we developed these senses at all, learnt to trust them?

All the factors listed above are at play when we are growing up and directly influence our lives. Not only how we see ourselves, but how we see others and the world around us. This becomes our blueprint for how to live. How we *think* we should live.

So how should we live? We have to accept, to begin with, that we are a product of our ancestors, our families, our schooling, our peers and our culture, and that it is only in later life, when we are older and more independent that we can go out and discover more for ourselves and, if we so choose, change our behaviours, our beliefs and our thinking. This is not easy, as any smoker trying to quit would tell you. If the change is not out of a necessity, in the form of a life threatening disease, or imminent danger, then as humans we seem quite content with the status quo. This is reflected in a general apathy for many of the worlds problems today. It is easy to defer to others, think of the problems as someone else's issue, or believe that you, as only one person, cannot make a difference.

However, change can take place, hence you are reading this book, have read others on self-improvement, life coaching, philosophy or religion, have gone on courses or retreats, watched hours of uplifting videos on the net, subscribed to a myriad of positive social media groups or websites that generate contemplative 'thoughts for the day', practice yoga or tai chi, meditate, or have a wooden heart on your wall that says *'Love is the answer!'* Excuse the flippancy, but hopefully you get my drift.

We want to change. We want to grow. Looking for answers is built into our DNA. The time seems to have passed when we just accept what we are told. There is too much that just doesn't fit, feel right or is just plain wrong. Fake news isn't news, it is just a lie, a fabrication; spin to influence our thinking, ultimately to either get us to like someone, buy something, or give away our money.

Are there answers in being spiritual or seeking a spiritual life? What does being spiritual really mean? Do you have to be spiritual to live a good and productive life? The truth of the matter is that you don't. Not a dictionary definition of being spiritual or religious. However we all have a spiritual side, even if that is just a joy for life and a caring heart beating inside us, that now and again we listen to. But isn't something so fundamental to so many people's lives, be they religious or not, worth investigating, just to be on the safe side?

Where are the tools and techniques to explore what spirituality means in a non-religious context, or what being connected to nature means, without having to become a farmer, tree surgeon or vet? As we urbanise, and spend more time in front of screens, our connection to nature and our relationship with the land has been eroded but, as much as we have been turning our backs upon it, we are linked to all life on this planet. From the air and water that sustains us, and the plant or animal based food that gives us energy, to the relationships we foster with the geography, be they cultivating the land, living in a certain village, town or city, or travelling along the roads and waterways, or across the oceans and skies.

Living in harmony with the land, the environment we find ourselves in, and the life we share it with (animal, vegetable and I would say mineral too) has always had its challenges. Ever since we first harnessed fire, we realised we could have some element of control of nature. Abusing this control has thrown us out of balance, given rise to power struggles, war and famine, disease and suffering, and more recently, with the increasing pace of industrialisation, forest decimation and wildlife species extinction. We know there is a problem, but what do we do about it? Again apathy and the feeling of *what can one person do?* may pervade. Well, one person can make an incredible difference, namely, and firstly, to themselves. That is where we all must start. Our relationship to ourselves.

Understanding more about who you are, who you want to be and looking to the areas that you wish to change about yourself is no easy task. However you can change and look at things differently. You can utilise tools and techniques similar to those used by your indigenous ancestors, work with the natural world and take great strides towards living the life you want to live. It is however a process, and yes there will be difficulties, hardships, perhaps even times of loneliness, fatigue and pain but the journey will be worthwhile, the rewards palpable.

The chance to live a life well lived shouldn't be taken lightly. You don't have to be anyone special, you don't have to achieve anything in particular, or reach a certain spiritual state, such as finding nirvana, heaven on earth or *touch the hand of God*. You just have to find that inner connection to life that has always been there, and always will be there. It was, and is, your birthright.

So how do you go about reclaiming your birthright? I am hoping that contained within these pages are ideas, exercises and practices that may help you. You do not have to follow them consecutively, or complete them all. However, please try and read through all of them and work with the ones that feel right for you. The ones that resonate with you. I suggest however that the following should not be missed out:

- Create your own spiritual altar
- Life CV
- Transmuting trauma
- Conduct your own memorial service for a loved one
- Ancestral lineage and cutting ties
- Inner child work
- Release using objects from nature.

If any of these sound daunting don't worry, that's just your instinctual defence to the unfamiliar kicking in and maybe also emotion inside beginning to bubble up. It's time to let it go and free yourself, ready for the next chapter in your life.

Part 1
Contemporary shamanism

"We are all visitors to this time, this place. We are just passing through. Our purpose here is to observe, to learn, to grow, to love…and then we return home."
Aboriginal proverb.

The Universe and *'what is'*

As much as we try to understand, categorise and describe the Universe, there is always something more, always something beyond our intellectual capability. But of course, that never stops us from trying to expand our knowledge. As Robert Browning put it;

"Ah but a man's reach should exceed his grasp,
or what's a heaven for?"

New discoveries and new scientifically arrived at facts are continually being unearthed, adding to and changing how we comprehend our planet and the Universe. However, as we look to return to the Moon, over fifty years since we first landed there, scientists now classify 95% of the Universe as dark energy and dark matter. That is, they do not know what else to call this missing stuff that must be there to fit the equations. At the other end of the scale the study of the small is throwing up new exotic energies and theories, such as in the field of quantum, changing how we understand interactions at a minute level. The Universe however is whole at this moment. It is behaving naturally. Science will say according to scientific laws and I believe that to be true. In the areas where we currently do not have a scientific explanation means only that the science is lagging behind. Maybe we do not have sensitive enough measuring devices, are not analysing the right data, or are perhaps not looking in the right area. A line from the poem Desiderata sums it up beautifully,

> *"And whether or not it is clear to you,*
> *no doubt the Universe is unfolding as it should."*

Science can tell us one thing but that picture is not complete. Nor will it ever be. Science, and our understanding of the Universe, will forever be expanding. We will never *know* it all. One can always look at a bigger or smaller level by developing more sensitive instruments or new detection methods. For example, discoveries at the quantum level are revealing new exotic particles, new building blocks for our model of how the Universe works. But these particles have always been there. Just because we had not seen them, could not detect their presence, or understand their influence, did not mean that they were not there.

Conversely we can always go bigger, probing further into the distance, looking deeper into space and therefore back in time. Seeing the light from a star that is five billion light years away means one is looking at radiation that was emitted five billion years ago. In fact, with the detection of the cosmic microwave background radiation we can look back to the dawn of the Universe and the Big Bang itself. Again, this radiation has always been there, even though it has only been discovered and labelled by the scientific community relatively recently. As the James Webb space telescope comes online, replacing the Hubble telescope as our most powerful eye on the night sky, we will really be able to look back to the dawn of time and, undoubtedly, some wonderful new discoveries will be made.

Gravity, similarly, has always been there. It may have been Isaac Newton (arguably on the back of Johannes Kepler and Robert Hooke's work) that gave us a mathematical formula to calculate gravity's strength, but there are references to a universal force, long before the European enlightenment. It is likely ancient civilisations understood that there was a *pull things down to earth* force. They may even have had their own word for it.

Much has been, and will continue to be, unearthed by science, however this will always be a subset of *"what is"*. In the diagram below *what is* represents all that is and ever will be. An all encompassing definition of everything. Everything known and unknown - all there is. There is nothing more outside of this boundary. Within this boundary is human knowledge - all that we as a species know and have ever known. The whole of human wisdom. As a subset of this we have science and what science knows to be true.

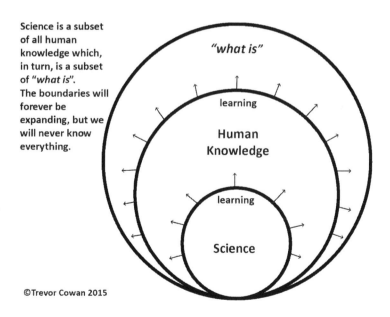

Science is a subset of all human knowledge which, in turn, is a subset of "what is". The boundaries will forever be expanding, but we will never know everything.

"what is"

learning

Human Knowledge

learning

Science

©Trevor Cowan 2015

There is knowledge and truth that lies outside the current limits of science, as yet unproven, maybe awaiting discovery by scientists. It is within this area that some ancient wisdom and indigenous knowledge sits. It is where various shamanic and spiritual practices reside, often on the boundary with science, sometimes far from it. This does not make them untrue. However, they will not stand up to scientific rigour and are therefore quickly (and understandably I might add) dismissed by the scientific and logical communities.

Nonetheless, useful knowledge, wisdom and truth, does not need a scientific stamp to make it valid. There is knowledge and wisdom that lies outside of the current (and ever expanding) boundary of science, truths yet to be unearthed or proven, and there is no reason why we can't tap into this well of wisdom. We are here today because our ancestors survived. They lived long enough to pass on their genes and raise a family. Hundreds and thousands of generations culminating in us, the most evolved humans ever. (Although as we look at the current state of the world some may argue of a recent devolution.) We can work in the realms beyond science, add to our own personal knowledge and experience, discover truths for ourselves and pass on our own teachings, just as people have done for millennia. Wisdom, ancient or otherwise, does not always fit inside the proven world of science.

Each day we understand more, unearthing new pieces to fit into the scientific jigsaw describing how the Universe works. One day we may have a fully scientific explanation of everything observed in the Universe, *The Theory of Everything*, as physicists call it, but I doubt that day will be tomorrow, or even one hundred years from now. So basing our total understanding of life on science, as accurate as it is, may not be showing us the whole picture. What is still missing from the picture of life, the Universe and everything...?

Shamanism and land connected cultures

Throughout human history there have been those that have lived in total connection to the planet, fostering a relationship to *Mother Earth* and the life upon her. Many indigenous peoples and tribal societies have lived in harmony with their environments, in tune with the natural rhythms and cycles, and knowing how to respect, nurture and honour the land. Within these communities there will be one or two individuals who have been called to go a little deeper with this Earth connection and become spiritual leaders of the community.

These people often have gone through tremendous trials to understand their place within their culture's spiritual framework and learnt to work with the energies of the land and the planet. Often they had traumatic or difficult upbringings and may even had been seen by the community as being mentally unbalanced to some degree. In modern parlance they did not fit in, had an alternative viewpoint on the world and were probably sensitive as a child - introverted, even exhibiting signs of autism or ADHD - but still creative, in their own way.

They have been given many names from shaman to mystic, soothsayer to healer, witch doctor to medicine woman, witch to wizard, priest to pastor. All have a connection to something bigger than just themselves and, when this realisation is made, they understand that it is their duty and life long path to develop their connection to earthly nature (or the *more-than-human world*, as first coined by David Abram[1]), help the community, honour and respect the land, and provide spiritual guidance for all who need it.

---

[1] David Abraham, *The Spell of the Sensuous*, 1996, Pantheon Books.

Shamanism, in all its forms, was the ancient method by which people understood the world and linked themselves to it. It was arguably the precursor to religion. Ancient shaman realised that there was an energy to all living things, a spirit if you will. This is easy to grasp when it comes to the spirit of an eagle, soaring up high above the canyon wall, but harder perhaps when it comes to the static nature of a tree and, more so, that of a rock. However, as science has proven, at the level of the very small, all things have a vibration, even rocks.

Over the years shamanism has taken many forms but has always been based upon an underlying spiritual connection to the land. It is not magic or mystical but real and useful, often like common sense, and to my mind, akin to an ancient form of psychology. The word shaman comes from the Siberian Evenk people as a general term for a tribal healer, with Core Shamanism being brought to the west by Michael Harner in the 1980s, and his book, *The Way of the Shaman*[2], becoming the bible for those that wished to embark on this path. It is from these roots contemporary shamanism became popular in the western world, as many people, myself included, were looking for answers to some of life's more esoteric questions, without the need to subscribe to a mainstream religion.

Of course, trying to describe, categorise and explain a mystical and spiritual tradition that has survived for millennia will never be clear cut. Everything is open to interpretation and each of us will naturally put our own take on the lessons, practices and teachings we take on board, as we follow our own paths.

Evolution is a slow process and our development as human beings has taken time. For millennia we were content living off the land and in our early nomadic culture, when resources ran low or the

---

[2] Michael Harner, *The Way of the Shaman*, 1980, Harper & Row.

weather conditions became unfavourable, we moved on. Eventually we settled, domesticated animals and farmed the land. The animals local to the community were revered and honoured, as they would provide food, clothing and tools (fish, boar, or deer for example), or be seen to be other worldly, such as the birds flying high above or aquatic creatures that survived underwater, unlike land based man. Making a spiritual connection to such seemingly miraculous creatures was not a surprise. Adorning oneself with clothing, head-dresses or ornaments made from these animals was symbolic of the respect the people had for them, and helped when worn in ceremony to embody the energies of these sacred animals.

We learnt to adapt to the seasons and stockpile resources for times of scarcity. Stories relating to many life experiences were passed down orally, generation after generation. From origin myths and survival techniques, to connecting with the more-than-human world and fostering community. The stories may have changed slightly over time, become a little embellished, but the inherent lessons, the teachings, stayed intact, because not only are the lessons proven, but the teacher knew it was his or her duty to keep them alive for future generations. Giving thanks for the knowledge passed on by our parents and grandparents was the norm, honouring them became routine, even ritualised.

Over time these practices and teachings were brought together into a syllabus, if you will, a group of lessons that were the spiritual medicine necessary for the individual and community to stay in balance and harmony with themselves, the land and the energies that pervaded all life. A medicine wheel of wisdom. Such medicine wheels are still prevalent today as the wisdom they contain is timeless.

The medicine wheel

The medicine wheel is a framework for spiritual teachings, often used by nature-based indigenous cultures (most commonly of the Americas), normally divided into the cardinal directions of north, south, east and west. Each *direction* has a specific set of teachings, with many medicine wheels using animal archetypes to represent and, to some degree, embody the energies and theme of that direction. The teachings of the medicine wheel offer the student a roadmap and the skills necessary to navigate it, to understand themselves more fully, comprehend their interactions with life on this planet and act as a gateway to being taught the tools necessary to become a contemporary shamanic practitioner.

There are a variety of medicine wheels (or similar frameworks for sharing knowledge) across the globe, with each indigenous peoples embracing their own version, based upon the local geography and their specific traditions passed down from generation to generation. Some practices will be well known and easily replicated whilst others will be difficult and require courage to undertake, with some even being kept secret within the community due to their sacredness or power.

However, there is often commonality to be found in the themes of each medicine wheel, namely letting go, facing fears, seeing the bigger picture, connection to the land, honouring yourself, honouring ancestors, stewardship of the planet, taking responsibility for your actions and celebrating the gift of life. These common themes are pertinent to all people on this planet and delving deeply into these areas can unearth great personal treasures.

A place for ceremony within modern life

In the modern western world we tend to live in our own space, alone or shared with a partner or family, in a house, bungalow, apartment or flat. The family unit is fluid and many young adults (if they can afford it) will leave home as soon as possible, with the ability and freedom to live almost anywhere on the planet. The majority of us do not live in tribal villages or small settlements any more, meaning there is a lot more detachment and isolation from others. This also means that community spaces, where people can come together and celebrate life, are being lost, leaving it to organised religions to provide such meeting places. What if you are not religious, either by not being raised with a faith or not being drawn to a religion? Where do you go for deep or sacred ceremony or ritual? The simple answer is to conduct them yourself, at home or in nature. Sadly we tend not to be drawn to ceremony that we carry out ourselves, mainly because we have never been taught how to, outside of a religious context. However, we probably undertake a variety of rituals without even realising it.

Rituals are actions that are repeated regularly or are part of a daily spiritual practice. They can be an informal process, such as how we go about our morning ablutions, or our method of making a cup of tea, to those that have a more symbolic meaning, such as lighting a candle before meditation, touching the earth before competing in a sporting event, or patting the door frame before leaving home. Sitting around the dinner table is a good example of a simple ritual. The family sharing what has happened in their day, connecting to each other, maybe giving thanks for the meal by saying grace.

A ceremony, on the other hand, is built around a specific purpose, such as a birth, marriage or funeral, but can also be used for personal spiritual connection and growth, in such areas as letting go, honouring nature, or connecting to the divine. In fact a ceremony can be held for pretty much anything. Recognising there are stages in life that people go through, problems we all face, and that there are difficulties that come with being human, is more important now than ever. Our issues, wounds and struggles are not the same as they were for our grandparents', or even our parents' generation. They have changed in-line with the rapid shifts we have seen globally over the past few decades. Ceremonies can help with dealing with these changes.

If you have been lucky enough to come from a good family, in a safe and resource rich country, then your ability to see challenges clearly, and deal with them effectively, has been given a good start. If your upbringing was not ideal, then there may be weaknesses in your ability to cope. This is where the support structures of family, friends and society should kick in, to provide buffers for these shortfalls. Not just plasters to cover the problem but real healing to get to the core issue, resolve it and unearth the wisdom of the lesson to be learnt.

This caring community side of life seems to have taken a back seat in the UK and the westernised world in general. Indigenous cultures, however, historically have this ingrained into their way of life. Be it sitting in a circle together in council, talking with elders, conducting rituals, honouring the ancestors, respecting each other, honouring the sacred feminine and masculine, or connecting to the spirit of the land. There would also be time devoted to just being in that child like state of wonderment and innocence that comes with truly seeing the beauty and majesty of the natural world.

This may seem like a long way from competitive urban city life where science, logic, money, efficiency and speed rule. But with some effort, and a re-establishment of the connection to nature, these gifts, these birth rights, can be reclaimed. Ceremony is a direct link to this connection. There are plenty of life events that mark transitions for us, such as birth, starting school, puberty, becoming a teenager, passing exams or graduating, reaching adulthood, marriage, a new home, new job, overcoming obstacles, retirement, and death. Conducting some form of ceremony can help recognise, honour and ease these transitions.

However, some rites of passage can seem barbaric to the modern world, especially if they involve pain or deprivation. For example, the Mawé people of the Amazon rainforest in Brazil, believe that any boy who wants to become a man must experience the worst pain the jungle has to offer, the sting of *Paraponera clavata*, the bullet ant. The boy must wear gloves that are woven with dozens of bullet ants for five minutes, enduring excruciating pain as the ants repeatedly sting him. Afterwards both hands and arms may be temporarily paralysed as a result of the ant venom, with the boy likely to suffer severe pain, convulsions or hallucinations, usually lasting for several days. The boys in this tribe may undergo this initiation process about twenty different times over a period of several months before they can be considered warriors. Such extreme ceremonies are unfamiliar to most people and I suggest are not necessary in the world in which most of us live.

A ceremony can also be used to let go of that part of your life that is ending, be it a career, a relationship, a home, a foodstuff, a habit, a pet, a treasured possession, even a way of life. If you feel like you are giving away something, losing something, then a small letting go ceremony can help the process and make you feel more at ease with the loss.

Ceremonies also act as a framework to conduct spiritual work, to bring something new into being, to ask for help with a current project, personal or global healing, guidance on life purpose, or to honour the changing seasons or moon cycles. A ceremony magnifies the potency of an intention and provides a narrative to help those present carry out what they have to do, a process where one is stepping away from the mundane and into the non-ordinary, stating to the Universe that something important is happening.

Of course ceremonies have become elaborate affairs, sometimes lasting hours, days or even weeks, with all manner of ceremonial trappings, from robes and elaborate wording, to sacred objects and religious relics. In truth, none of these are necessary, although admittedly the wearing of ritualistic garments or using sacred objects can feel powerful and put one in the right frame of mind for conducting the ceremony. However, many ceremonies have developed and evolved over time and, mainly due to the male egos involved, have often become overly ornate, decorative and, at times, rigid in their structure.

All that is really necessary is an opening intention, doing the spiritual work and ending in gratitude.

Part 2
Shamanic Engineering

"Shamanism is not a course, but a life journey"
Alberto Villoldo.

Framework used

Shamanism, contemporary or otherwise, can only be touched upon in a book. If you wish to go deeper with shamanic work then you will need a teacher to work with directly, ideally studying with others so that experiences can be shared. Often there is as much to be learnt from the other people in a group as from the teacher. Actively seeking out help and authentic training is an acknowledgement that you are serious in your endeavours. It is similar for the exercises described in this book. Actively engaging in them will result in a more profound experience, over and above any comprehension from just reading.

As previously mentioned the medicine wheel is a framework for spiritual teachings, often used by nature-based indigenous peoples. There are numerous medicine wheels (or similar systems) around the world, each varying due the geography and different cultures they represent. However, even with these differences, sometimes dramatic (think of Inuit geography compared to that of Australian aboriginal), they often have similar core teachings and practices, as the human relationship with the natural world and life's general issues are common themes.

The exercises and activities in this book are to some extent based upon the medicine wheel of the Q'ero paqos (spiritual leaders) of the Peruvian highlands, as taught to me by my shamanic teacher Skie Hummingbird, and using the same South American animal archetypes of snake, jaguar, hummingbird and condor.

The essence of these teachings, and teachings from various other shamanic traditions encountered on my travels, are interwoven with my lessons from many years of working directly with nature and the energies therein, to provide a practical and effective framework for individual self discovery, growth and a re-connection to nature and the world around us (leaving aside any creation stories, survival skills or community actions.) However, again please note, out of respect for my shamanic lineage I am not sharing within this book any sacred teachings or practices that should be taught directly. I would only pass on such teachings as part of a shamanic practitioner training course. There may, however, be some similarities or cross over in some of the exercises, due to the common goal of self discovery and connecting to nature.

The core of this book is split into seven sections (*the Directions*), representing the different areas of self exploration and teaching. The four cardinal directions, *South, West, North and East,* followed by sections entitled *Mother Earth, Father Sky* and *The Centre.*

- *The South* is concerned with looking at the past and letting go; it is represented by Serpent.
- *The West* is working with death and facing fears; it is represented by Jaguar.
- *The North* is about magic, seeing the joy in life and honouring the ancestors; it is represented by Hummingbird.

- *The East* involves seeing the bigger picture; it is represented by Eagle or Condor.

- *Mother Earth* is acknowledging our connection to all life on this planet. All that is below.

- *Father Sky* represents that which is *beyond* ourselves, our connection to the Universe, God/Goddess or Great Spirit. All that is above.

- *The Centre* represents ourself; the responsibility we have standing in sovereignty at the centre of our own medicine wheel.

My teacher, Skie, put it like this:

"Serpent clears the ground, Jaguar takes you deeper into your own personal jungle, Hummingbird moves you higher and seeks out the beauty and flowers, Eagle rises above it all. They are different perspectives of the same thing, ourselves and our journey through life. One is not better than the other. There is no hierarchy. When completed we can sit in the middle, and maybe visit The West from an eagle perspective. The wheel will help reorganise your life, any patterns and behaviours, in line with what is best for you."

The exercises provided may, in some instances, seem more suited to the psychologist's couch, as shamanism is, in my opinion, akin to an ancient form of psychology. In fact, I would say psychology today has its roots in shamanism. The two are related because they are both about connection. Connection to the self, to others and to that which is beyond our consciousness, be it our sub-consciousness, a super or collective consciousness, universal energy, a creation energy, planetary energy, spirit or the divine. Working through any self help book is, by definition, working psychologically.

Basic tool kit

You probably already have many of the *tools* suggested, but if not they are readily available at little or no expense. There is no need to have special objects; ones with a high value, deemed sacred, blessed by a guru, or from a far off exotic land. Of course we are often drawn to beautiful or interesting objects and that is fine. Trust your intuition. Remember though, the phrase "a bad workman always blames his tools", is just as pertinent in the spiritual and shamanic world as in any other.

Items required:

- A journal. It is a good idea to have a journal to write in, as noting your thoughts and experiences pertinent to your journey can act as way markers in the future, when you look back at the path you have taken and see just how far you have come.

- Sustainably sourced incense, sage or palo santo[3] wood, for burning and smudging.

- A smudge fan. Usually made from feathers, to waft smoke from burning sage or palo santo. A single feather found in nature can be used.

- Hand drum and/or rattle. At some point you will want a rattle or hand drum, but initially they are not required as recordings are available online. A rattle is easier to hold and use, and cheaper and less intrusive regarding noise than a drum, but either is fine. Ideally you want to try these items to make sure they sound right for you.

---

[3] Palo Santo (*Bursera Graveolens)* is a native tree of Central and South America. Its name translates as "holy tree" with the wood producing a highly fragrant smoke when burnt.

- Fifteen and thirty minute drumming and/or rattling audio files. These should be instrumental only. Available online.

- A blindfold to enter darkness, ideally a Mindfold (a foam padded mask with eye cut outs for comfortable wearing) or similar.

- A small stick, about 30cms (12 inches) long. It should be strong enough to withstand some flexing but light enough for you to hold in one hand and tap over your body when laying down. It should *feel* right when you hold it. Whittle it, remove sharp edges or overly rough bark and knots, smooth it with sandpaper, or keep it totally natural. Make it yours. (See the section on trees and wood.)

- Candles or tea lights.

- A self supporting mirror that you can look into when sitting down.

- A small compass, so that you know the cardinal directions wherever you are - often available on a smartphone.

- Audio/mp3 player (a smartphone is ideal) and headphones.

Where possible, ensure these items are ethically and sustainably sourced.

Space to work

The exercises and processes described in this book are called *work*, as that is what they are, work upon yourself. Therefore you need a space to carry out this work. Ideally you will have a room or area that can be dedicated to this. A place of calm and tranquillity, where you can sit or lay down and not be disturbed. It doesn't have to be a separate room, but this helps. It could be your bedroom, study or conservatory, perhaps even a shed, or separate building outside. Make this space meditative by decorating it appropriately, maybe adorning the walls with artwork that calms and inspires you. Create a relaxed ambience by lighting a candle, burning quality incense, sage or palo santo wood, or playing calming background music. There are no rules, this is your space. Update how it looks as often as you like, especially when you are drawn to do so.

Spiritual altar

This is a place, normally a low lying table or shelf, covered with a beautiful cloth if you wish, where you keep your spiritual and sacred objects. You probably have a place, or even a number of places, where you already put photos or meaningful objects. Try collecting them together to form your own spiritual altar, locating it in your meditative space, so you can sit with it undisturbed and easily gaze upon the objects, or choose one to meditate with. It can contain any objects or pictures that are relevant to you and your own take on spirituality; religious objects, natural objects, trinkets and keepsakes, crystals, stones, carvings, photos of loved ones, totems, mandalas, etc. Anything that feels important, beautiful or sacred to you. Review it and change it as you see fit. It should be dynamic and reflect your own personal spiritual journey.

Opening sacred space

Whenever shamanic or spiritual work is being undertaken, especially in a new environment, you should take a moment to set the scene and *open* the space where you will be working. This is known as opening sacred space. It is a form of prayer and a way of asking for help from that which is outside of yourself, be it the more-than-human world, God/Goddess, spirit, the Universe, or maybe even just your own subconscious. If you are going to ask for help why not ask for help from all around you? From the four cardinal directions north, east, south and west, from below and from above? This is my method (and the one I was first taught), accompanied by a short prayer as I face each direction; kneeling on the ground for the *below* and standing, raising my hands over my head, for the *above*. I noticed when first doing this that I felt awkward, raising my hands up as I asked for help from whatever is above, most often called Great Spirit, God or the Universe. My rational background in science and engineering meant I had not encountered or believed in anything like this before, so I felt a little fraudulent, as I still did not have any evidence of a higher power. Not tangible evidence anyway. But I was in training. I was drawn to this path and to the teachings, so I went with it. As I progressed and opened up, my viewpoint altered. Opening space became easier, felt more natural and also more powerful.

Perhaps the biggest change was the humbling effect it had. When I really started to mean the words of the prayer, I found emotions could move easily within me and great releases would take place, just by opening space. Realising I needed spiritual guidance, feeling worthy of receiving such guidance, trusting that the help would come and recognising that, to some degree, I was part of a long lineage of people who have asked for and received such help, was at times a little overwhelming, but truly humbling.

It makes sense to me that asking for help from all around is the best and most all encompassing method. But you can use many other methods to open space, such as casting a circle with your finger, imagining helping energy coming to you from all around, or asking for spirit, God, the Universe, or whatever you are drawn to, to come and be with you. Even just sitting next to your altar, kneeling at the foot of your bed in prayer, or in a chair before meditation, asking in your mind for help, is sufficient if you deem it so. As with many practices it is the intention that counts.

If you are cynical about working with (or believing in) God, spirit, or any other form of intelligence or energy outside of yourself, why not accept that you are at least working with your subconscious. That part of your higher functioning that is continually operating, even if *you*, the conscious you, is blissfully unaware of it. Think of it as being similar to the physical processes happening constantly within your body that your consciousness is oblivious to, such as your digestive, endocrine, or cardiovascular systems (unless, of course, there is a problem.) Accept that your subconscious (and perhaps a super consciousness) is at work whilst your consciousness gets on with day to day living and the experience of being *you*.

Asking for help is fine, accepting it is another matter. Our egos can be very powerful and manipulative. Be careful not to fall into the ego trap of equating what you put in to what you expect to receive out. For example, praying twelve hours a day will not necessarily bring greater results than a short two minute prayer in the morning. Adorning statues of deities with flowers, food, alcohol, or beautiful trinkets doesn't mean you deserve to be rewarded with a spiritual gift. It is not an equation to be manipulated.

The ego can also filter and distort information and sensory input, becoming a barrier to any help that may be forthcoming, by dismissing it as fictitious, fanciful or irrelevant. To limit the ego's effect, try putting yourself into a child like state when undertaking spiritual work. That is, put yourself into a state of not knowing. One of awe and wonder and, most importantly, in a place of play. Playing is one of the most powerful ways children (and most young mammals) learn the skills they will need in adulthood. It is no different in the spiritual arena, as spiritually we are all children. If we were advanced then the world would not be in the state it is today.

So opening sacred space is talking to the unknown, or even the unknowable. It is talking to that which is beyond our consciousness, to that which we are normally unaware of, saying that we are here and ready to do some meaningful work, whilst humbly realising that we do not know it all and, like a child, we would like some help.

Here is a simple opening space prayer from the book *Rolling Thunder*, by Doug Boyd[4].

> *"Turn to each direction, look up and down,*
> *and ask for help.*
> *to the east where the Sun rises*
> *to the north where the cold come from*
> *to the south where the light comes from*
> *to the west where the Sun sets*
> *to father Sun*
> *to mother earth."*

The prayer I generally use to 'call in' the directions is shown below. It was gifted to me by my teacher who, in turn, received it from her teacher. This version is for use within a group setting but can work individually too. I have modified the wording slightly over the years

---

[4] Doug Boyd, *Rolling Thunder*, 1974, Random House.

and would rattle briefly, or give a couple of drum beats, before saying the words to each direction, turning ninety degrees to face each, going down to the earth, or reaching up to the sky.

To the winds of the South,
Energies and spirits of the South,
Great Serpent come,
Come wrap your coils of golden light around us.
Teach us to shed our skin the way you shed yours, to let go
Teach us how to walk softly upon this earth.
Show us the beauty way.

To the winds of the West,
Energies and spirits of the West,
Mother, sister Jaguar come, come from your lair.
Protect this medicine space.
Show us the way of peace,
To live impeccably.
Show us the way beyond our fears,
Beyond death.

To the winds of the North,
Energies and spirits of the North,
Royal Hummingbird come,
Show us the magic and joy there is in life.
Share with us your courage and dogged determination,
To keep following our epic journey,
Even if, at times, it means going sideways or backwards.
And ancestors, grandmothers, grandfathers,
Come, warm your hands by our fires,
Whisper to us upon the wind.
We honour those that have gone before us,
And those to come after us, our children's children.

To the winds of the East,
Energies and spirits of the East,
Great Eagle, Condor, come from your mountain top,
Protect us under your wing.
Teach us to fly high, to soar, to see beyond.
Show us the mountains we only dare dream of,
Our heart's true calling,
And teach us to fly wing to wing with the Great Spirit.

Mother Earth, Pachamama, our home,
We gather for the healing of all your children.
The ancient stone people,
The healing plant people,
The four legged, the two legged, the creepy crawlies,
The winged, the finned and the furred ones,
The sliders and slitherers,
The burrowers and cave dwellers,
our brothers and sisters,
All our relations.

Grandmother Moon, Grandfather Sky,
Star nations, God, Goddess, the divine,
Great Spirit, Great Mystery,
Consciousness, super-consciousness,
You who are known by a thousand names and you who are
the unnameable one,
Thank you for bringing us together and
Thank you for allowing us to sing this song of life.

The most important part of any prayer is intention and feeling, so choose words that resonate with you.

Closing sacred space

If you are going to open sacred space before any ceremonial or spiritual work, then it makes sense that once completed the space should be closed. This can be achieved simply by a thank you to each of the directions, to any energies, consciousness, or spirits you may have invited or felt the presence of and a general heartfelt moment of gratitude for any teachings that have come to you during the session. Closing space also acts to signify that you have finished your work in/with the non-ordinary world and are now returning to or re-entering the ordinary world again.

Opening sacred space whilst on the move

You do not have to be in a fixed position to open sacred space. It can be opened at one point and closed at another if, for example, you are out walking in nature. Think of opening space as creating a gateway which you can pass through and then, as you continue your walk, carry out your spiritual work, walk in meditation, or just connect with the nature around you. When finished close this gateway by closing space, even if you are ten miles from where you opened it. In a crowded public place you may want to use minimal movements to open space, maybe just turning briefly to each of the directions, touching the ground and gazing to the sky as you recite your prayer softly under your breath.

Grounding

Much of the spiritual work described in this book involves visualisation and connecting with something outside of yourself, or your consciousness, in one way or another. When the work has been completed one can sometimes feel light headed or a little disconnected. Normally spiritual work carried out in nature is by its very essence grounding, but if you have not been *working* outside then taking time to reconnect to the earth, to ground yourself, is worthwhile, as it helps bring you back into your body and be able to continue with your day without a floaty or *not all there* feeling.

Grounding is especially important for people who spend a lot of time in their mind, due to their employment or lifestyle, or are detached from the land for long periods of time. As more of us live in urban environments, and in flats or apartments, then our connection to the land and the natural world is being eroded. Conversely those that live in the country, work with the land, or spend a lot of time in nature, will probably find that grounding is not necessary, as it happens naturally due to their already strong connection to the earth.

The simplest method to ground is to stand up and imagine roots growing out of your feet and being sent down deep into the earth. It doesn't matter if you are wearing shoes or away from the ground (i.e. on the 23rd floor of a building), just imagine the roots going down from wherever you are into the earth. Visualise the roots going deep and spreading out in all directions, connecting you to the planet. This is often enough but if you want to go further visualise an energy, maybe in the form of a colour, coming up the roots from the earth into your feet and body, energising and strengthening your earth connection. Breathe this in on the in-breath and let go of any negativity or disconnect on the out-breath. A few cycles of breathing should be enough to feel *back in your body* and grounded.

Having a warming drink or something to eat is also grounding and especially worthwhile if there were major shifts during your session.

Visualising and using your imagination

Many of the exercises described in this book call for some form of visualisation, a way of seeing things in your mind by imagining scenarios or events, and perhaps at times, merging these with actual memories. Being relaxed and in darkness (by using a blindfold) can help with visualising, as can the use of a repetitive drum beat or rattle.

Visualisations are not only used in healing therapies but also in many areas of self improvement where a goal is to be achieved; from sports people visualising themselves winning, to politicians rehearsing public speaking engagements, or entrepreneurs envisaging a successful business. The power of visualising and creating a success in your mind is not to be underestimated.

However not everybody imagines or visualises in the same way. In fact, some people find it very difficult to *see* things in their mind. So try this exercise. Imagine an orange. Now imagine it cut in half and imagine the smell, perhaps even the taste. Get your juices flowing. Now imagine an elephant. Imagine it standing on an orange. Shrink the elephant. Make the orange big. Can you change the elephant from grey to orange, and the orange from orange to grey? Try imagining the orange's flesh as purple, the outer skin silver and, instead of pips, visualise diamonds dotted within the segments. If you can imagine this, you can imagine anything, with a little bit of effort. On the other hand, if you found this exercise difficult then work with your other senses. Maybe you can feel or sense a situation or scenario, can actually taste the orange for example, or hear the elephant. Also look at how you recall dreams and use this method when asked to visualise in the exercises. Trust that whatever way you imagine is right for you.

Shamanic journeying

In the shamanic view there is a non-ordinary reality beyond our normal physical world that can be accessed by using shamanic journeying. All indigenous cultures have their own ways to journey and their own non-ordinary landscapes to journey within, such as *The Dreamtime* in the Australian aboriginal tradition or *The Otherworld* in Celtic shamanism.

Shaman go into a trance like state when they go on a journey to connect with their spiritual allies. They enter an altered trance state with the use of a repetitive drumbeat, rattle, or song, sometimes aided by medicine plants (see *Mother Earth* section). The journeying I am describing here, is slightly different, namely a form of active meditation. Meditation takes the meditator away from their thoughts, giving them a break from the usual mind chatter. Shamanic journeying is far more of a dialogue, used to obtain information and find answers to questions. It is a dialogue with, if nothing else, your psyche or subconscious, and normally filled with metaphor and symbolism, often more concrete than that of a dream.

To journey effectively one needs to occupy the part of the mind that wants input. In meditation this can be achieved by using a mantra, repeating it over and over to create an almost trance like state, or by focusing on the breath, noting the coolness of the air entering the nostrils on the in-breath, and the warmth of it on the out breath. In shamanic journeying a similar *distraction* is needed, but in this case it is a constant beat or pulse, most commonly provided by a drum or rattle. A blissful trance like state can be achieved when allowing this beat to act as a focal point for the mind and become the heartbeat of the journey. In shamanism the drum is often referred to as having horse energy or spirit, as it is upon this beat that the practitioner *rides* and is transported to *other* places.

Going into darkness is a key part of journeying, either with one's eyes closed, by wearing a blindfold, or by venturing into a dark place. Caves, or especially constructed dark chambers, such as sweat lodges or kivas[5], were (and are) used by shaman and spiritual workers to journey to the non-ordinary world and conduct their own rituals and ceremonies. However, accessibility to caves and dark spaces in the modern world is limited, but one can make a room practically lightproof with a little effort, by using blackout curtains combined with a window plug, made from cardboard, foam, or similar, and rolled up towels for any gaps at the bottom of doorways.

Finally, setting an initial intention is a good practice, so that there is a definite purpose for the journey. This can help guide the journey and is something to focus upon when, as is often the case, one maybe distracted by a noise back in the ordinary world, or hijacked by a stray thought about dinner, for example, and brought out of the journey. As with meditation, let such thoughts and distractions pass, return focus to your intention and allow yourself to be taken away again on the beat of the drum. With this constant beat you can visualise scenarios, keeping in mind your intention, and journey to seek information and answers to your questions.

Shamanic practitioners will use journeying to connect with their spirit guides. These can take any form, be they human like, ethereal beings, or known or fantastical animals. Quite commonly it is animal spirits that are consulted, because as humans we have a strong emotional, physical and evolutionary relationship with the animal kingdom. In the journey within this non-ordinary reality, there are no physical rules. We can explore any place, go to any time, be comfortable in any environment and be visited by any manner of being or animal, communicate with them and be taken on a journey with these spiritual allies as our guides.

---

[5] a kiva is chamber, built wholly or partly underground, traditionally used for religious rites.

Types of shamanic journey

There are generally three types of journey in the shamanic practitioner's tool kit; namely the lower, middle and upper world journeys.

A lower world journey can be helpful with past events, to access your subconscious and work on personal transformation at a soul level. It begins by visualising yourself going downwards, normally through an opening in the earth, such as an animal burrow, a cave, a rock crevice or tree root, maybe even down a waterfall, into a well, or into the ocean depths. It is normally a place where helping animal spirits can be found. A literary example of a lower world journey is Lewis Carol's *Alice in Wonderland*, where Alice has her adventures after going down a rabbit hole.

An upper world journey is about connecting to your higher self, seeking guidance from spiritual teachers, be they ascended masters, gurus, or the divine. It is a place for personal enlightenment and to see future possibilities. The journey begins with taking yourself upwards, be it climbing a tree, rope or ladder, jumping skywards from the top of a mountain, soaring up in a hot air balloon, or being taken away by a tornado, like Dorothy's journey to Oz. The journey continues upwards breaking through layers or boundaries until the non-ordinary upper world is discovered, often a fantastical place amongst the heavens. There may be gates to be passed through, giving access to a celestial world, often with a castle or city in the sky; an Emerald city in the case of *The Wizard of Oz*. Another literary example is Jack climbing the beanstalk, discovering his upper world is home to a giant. If the lower world journey is earthly and nature based, the upper world journey is ethereal and otherworldly. More often than not, the spiritual allies encountered in the upper world are more human in nature, but this is not a rule.

Additionally when one sets out on a journey to one world, the journey may take you to another. This is fine. Just trust you are visiting the right place and allow the journey unfold.

The middle world journey takes place in this realm, in places that are familiar to you. It is a journey to understand your place right now within the world, and to connect with the nature that inhabits it. The visualisation is simply to be in a place you know, such as your garden or local park, and commune with the plants or trees there. This type of journey can be done, for example, when sat on a bench in the park to connect with the flora and fauna of the place.

These three worlds are often symbolised by a 'World Tree', also known as the *axis mundi*. The tree has roots going down into the earth representing the lower world (gut feel, connection to soul, for help with emotions deep within yourself), the trunk is the middle world (here and now, reflecting back to us at eye level, easy to touch) and the branches reach high towards the upper world (asking for help from guides or teachers, outside of ourselves, our higher self).

There are plenty of online resources or books on the subject of shamanic journeying if you want to understand more and, like with all activities, your confidence will grow with practice.

General outline of a short shamanic journey

This is a general outline that you can read through to become familiar with and try for yourself, but there are also recorded journeys available online (or on my website, *ShamanicHelp.org*) with narration that you can follow.

You will need an intention for the journey. What is it that you want to work upon? A couple of simple intentions are, *What do I need to know today?* or *What is my spirit animal?*, but they can be deeper, depending on your level of experience with journeying. Animals, our relationship to them, and the energy or spirit they embody, are a cornerstone of shamanic philosophies, with a spirit or totem animal being one that we have a connection with (sometimes lifelong) and whose spirit wants to be with us to teach or show us something.

Be in a peaceful, safe space where you are not going to be disturbed. Laying down or sitting comfortably is fine. Use headphones to listen to a shamanic drumming instrumental audio file, no longer than thirty minutes. Set the volume to your own comfort level, but I suggest having it so that the drumming is in the background and not drowning out your thoughts. Make use of a blindfold or similar to go into darkness. Relax, take some calming breaths and begin listening to the drum beats.

Start by visualising yourself laying down in a beautiful place in nature, maybe a real place, a place you know from your childhood, or a place that is totally fictitious. It doesn't matter. Take a moment to feel the grass or ground under you, supporting you. Feel safe here.

Notice the smells, the sights and the sounds of nature around you. Feel the warmth of the Sun on your face and body. Breathe it all in. Feel at peace, feel supported, feel relaxed. Spend time acclimatising and becoming familiar with this place in your mind.

When you are ready, visualise yourself standing up from this spot in nature and start walking. See a path ahead of you and walk upon it. Notice the sound of your footsteps on the path. After a short while see a wooded area up ahead. Follow the path into the trees. Notice the change in sounds, temperature and smell. Keep walking through the trees until you see the path open out into a clearing. Enter the clearing and see a stone circle in the centre. A circle of stones about ten metres / ten yards across. Walk to the circle and step into the middle of it. It is from within this circle that you can focus on your intention and deepen your journey.

The journey will be dependent on what you have intended and can be as simple as asking to meet your spirit animal, or deeper work such as connecting with ancestors, cutting past ties, or meeting the divine. This stone circle is a safe and sacred space. A place to do spiritual work. Be humble in this place as you are asking for help; help to gain insight, shed something that no longer serves you, or help to grow. Be respectful but do not lose the child like wonder and awe of being in a magical place. Be open and allow whatever that wants to come up, to come up. If there is emotion, don't fight it, go into it, let it come out and release it. You may leave the circle on your journey, be transported somewhere else or be taken to another place. You may even find yourself transformed into an animal or a non-human being as part of the journey. All of this is OK as you can be anything, communicate with everything, go anywhere and to any time, whilst in this liminal place.

For an upper world journey start by going up in some way from the stone circle, for a lower world journey go down initially. However, within each journey you can be taken away in any direction. This can seem confusing but as long as your intention was clear at the beginning then let the journey unfold as it wants. We shall use the intention to meet your spirit (or totem) animal, so whilst in the stone circle look for a way to go down into the earth; for example, through an animal burrow. Feel yourself go down into the earth, pushing through the ground and forcing your way through a tunnel. After a period see a light at the end of the tunnel and pop out into your lower world. This can take on any appearance but is normally a beautiful natural landscape. You may even find yourself back in your stone circle, which is fine.

From this place call out and ask for your spirit animal to come to you. See, feel or imagine an animal coming to you from the trees, the air or the ground. There may be many. Ask each one in turn if it is your spirit animal? If it says "no", or doesn't feel right, then thank it for coming and ask again for your spirit animal to come to you. When you feel you have the right one ask it some questions. Maybe find out it's name and ask why has it come to you? What does it want to show you? It is likely your spirit animal will want to take you on a journey and you may even find yourself transforming into the same animal, deepening the connection. Go with them, knowing it is safe to go wherever, and to whenever, they wish to take you. Give yourself permission to drift and flow with the intention you made and explore the landscape of your journey as it unfolds in your mind, in your psyche, in your feelings, or however you are experiencing it. The more fully you can immerse yourself in this the better. If at any point you come out of the journey, i.e. your thoughts drift onto something else back in the ordinary world, gently bring your awareness back to the drum beat and focus back on your intention and the journey.

When the you hear the *call back* of the drum, (the drum beat will stop, pulse a few times and then become fast), it is time to start coming back as the journey is coming to an end. Return to the stone circle if you have left it, giving thanks to any animals, people, or spirits that came to you during the journey, or for any teachings or messages received. Step out of the stone circle, back across the clearing, along the path through the trees, returning to your place in nature and laying back down.

Allow the shamanic drumming to finish and slowly bring yourself back to your senses in the ordinary world by wiggling your fingers and toes, removing any blindfold and slowly opening your eyes. Be in gratitude again, as you slowly return to your physical body. Journalling any thoughts, messages received or insight given is often useful.

In the time after, the following minutes, hours or even days, you may see signs pertinent to your journey in the ordinary world. These can take the form of an image, a sound or a situation that resonates deeply with the journey you have just been on. These signs are gifts from the Universe/God/Goddess/spirit, showing that your efforts have not gone to waste and that you have been listened to. One such example is seeing a newly revealed spirit animal appear in a magazine, on a billboard poster, on TV or the internet, when you weren't actively looking for it. You might even receive contact out of the blue from a person that was in your journey.

Maybe look at such coincidences as confirmation that you are part of something much bigger.

The shamanic process

If you are undertaking any shamanic or deeply spiritual work the below can act as a generalised outline of the process to be followed.

- Be in a safe, comfortable space where you can work undisturbed, with your tools to hand.
- Mute your phone.
- Create the right atmosphere. Maybe light a candle, smudge the area and yourself, or put on some background music.
- Set an intention for the work you are about to undertake.
- Open sacred space.
- Feel the connection to those that you have called in, be they ancestors, animal totems, spiritual beings, a higher consciousness, the divine, etc.
- Do the work based on your intention. Remember to be playful and in child like openness.
- Use your tools or a drumming audio file/cd to help with journeying and visualisation.
- Allow any releasing to happen. Do not block it. Tapping the belly, heart or throat areas with your fingers or stick can help the release.
- When finished ensure some form of healing or soothing energy is pulled in to fill up any gaps left by the releasing, i.e. visualise golden sunlight or silver moonlight filling your whole body. Gently place your hands where you feel they are needed to help direct this healing energy or light.

- Spend some time in stillness, whilst being in a place of gratitude.

- Close the space.

- Ensure you are grounded afterwards, feeling ready to continue with your day.

- Journal your experience for future reference.

- Keep an eye (and ear) open, for any signs from the Universe pertinent to the work you have just completed, over the following days. Use your intuition to discern a clear sign from noise.

All of the tools and techniques outlined in this section are aimed to help you with the work on yourself in the following chapters. Do not worry about making mistakes, missing something out, or doing an exercise differently. Having the intention and being open, humble and in gratitude afterwards are all that is really needed.

Warning and disclaimer

Working on yourself is difficult and not for the feint of heart. You have to be prepared to face yourself, "warts and all" as they say. Doing the exercises on your own will require strength and determination. This is why the exercises and contemporary shamanic practices outlined are described as *work*, because they are work, work upon yourself. You may feel that some of the exercises are better to do with another person, or with the help and guidance of a trained shamanic practitioner. If you are drawn to working with another then please do so, as this can help you feel supported when going fully or more deeply into the process, but do try them at least once on your own first.

Be ready to reassess and even reject what you have previously learnt, some of which may be deeply ingrained. Trying to change 'a habit of a lifetime' is tricky at best. This can lead to a grief process, grief for the loss of what has previously been held onto as truth. Be prepared for this. Grief is OK. Sadness is OK. In fact any human emotion is fine. What is important is not to dwell in the negative emotions. Let them be springboards to a more illuminated, connected and authentic life.

Please be aware that I am not a trained medical professional. Any of the exercises or advice in this book should not replace professional healthcare or the guidance of your doctor.

Note also that there are exercises shared that offer some degree of danger when undertaken, such as working with darkness, working with and under water, working with fire and even looking towards the Sun with the eyes closed. I am confident that common sense will prevail when trying any of the exercises but I have to say that you carry out any of these practices at your own risk. Be sensible and err on the side of caution, but please at the same time have fun and play with the ideas, as playing is how we really learn. Potentially dangerous exercises are marked with **Note: Safety warning**. Please heed this.

Some of the exercises or practices can be done anywhere; on the bus, the train, or sat on a park bench. Most though require some action and contemplation or visualisation, so your focus will often be elsewhere. Therefore, as the normal disclaimers say, do not try any of these exercises whilst driving or operating heavy machinery. Or light machinery for that matter!

Part 3
The Directions

The South - Healing the past

"Who looks outside, dreams. Who looks inside, awakes."
Carl Jung.

The direction of *The South* is represented by Serpent within the medicine wheel used as a general framework for this book. It is about letting go of what has gone before. Shedding the past, just as a snake sheds its skin. Our past affects us in many ways, so the following exercises will help clarify your own history and illuminate where the focus of your inner work should be.

Life CV

In your journal, or even in a computer spread sheet, write down in the left column a consecutive list of the years you have been alive, starting from a year before you were born to the current year (2022 at time of writing). For example if you born in 1971 write:

1970
1971 - born
1972
1973
...
2022

In this case the list would be fifty-two lines long. Against the year before you were born write down any major world event that was happening around the time of your conception, or the situation your parents were going through during that period. Were they together, in love, married? Do you know? If not why not ask them? If they have passed is there another family member you can ask? If not try to meditate or journey on this and ask to be shown more information. Against each of the other years fill in key or major events in your life. Start with the most impactful events such as traumas, births, deaths, relationships, illnesses, etc. Then add other life events, such as moving home, pets, schools attended, memorable vacations, in fact anything that comes to your mind. If it comes to mind, it is worth writing down. Anything you feel had, or could have had, an effect upon you mentally, physically or emotionally. You may also want to include material objects, possessions or keepsakes, TV shows or movies, books, magazines or posters, etc., that you remember affecting or influencing you.

Keep the list relatively handy so that you can add to it whenever something important comes to mind, because it is unlikely you will remember everything in one sitting.

What emotions have been brought up by writing this list? Is there anything remembered that surprises you, anything that you feel is still an issue? Any major life event has an influence on us. It can shape us in one way or another. There are lessons to be learnt from such an event. Why did it happen? How did it change the course of our life? What strength have we drawn from it? How can our experience help others? As creatures of habit there are patterns in our daily lives. Are there any patterns in your *Life CV*? Does anything keep repeating? An example of a common relationship pattern stems from the expression, "I seem to always date this type of person", often spoken with a sigh of resignation.

Not all traumas or upheavals in our lives are obvious. Yes there is clear influence from the major events, now listed on your *Life CV*, but others can be hidden and could have been playing out within our lives at a level we are unaware of. Often these stem from events in our childhood and ones that perhaps we give little or no credence towards. The death of a pet when we are young is par for the course in most children's lives but what if it had an underlying effect on us, one that carries through into adulthood? Are we aware of this? Then there are the echoes of what we have inherited from our parents and their bloodline, both genetically and perhaps also energetically. Fortunately these less obvious influences upon our character and life patterns can still be accessed and worked upon at a deeper level, although some may require the assistance of a shamanic practitioner or similar to unlock them.

Additionally, as we all have at least one book inside us, your *Life CV* can act as a basis for your autobiography!

Letting Go

Trauma and wounds from the past can often be held onto and, over time, we begin to believe that this is part of who we are. The scars are like badges. Badges that say what we have been through, what we have survived, how tough we are. Over the years these scars become part of us and, like prized possessions, letting them go becomes difficult. Denial creeps in as to how much they actually effect us. It is not until one really starts digging into these wounds that the true power of the trauma can be unearthed. Going to a psychiatrist or similar therapist is the normal route; spending hours *on the couch*, talking and chipping away at the issue, possibly re-framing it, and hopefully being given the tools to understand and move on from the problem in a healthy way. But I believe the shamanic method is a faster, more profound and fuller experience, that also opens up a new pathway to understanding yourself, the world and your place within it - which, to my mind, is the whole point of any psychiatric endeavour anyway. The word psychiatry has it's roots in ancient Greek; *psych* from *psykhē*, meaning 'soul', and *-iatry* from *'iātrikos'*, meaning 'medical treatment', and *'iāsthai'*, meaning 'to heal'. Therefore psychiatry literally means 'medical treatment of the soul', or 'heal the soul'. To my mind 'heal the soul' sounds like work that involves the spiritual rather than just the mental or psychological. Please note I am not dismissing psychiatric help and once again state that the exercises in this book should not replace any medical treatment being received, or the advice of trained healthcare professionals, but rather be used as complimentary and for the purpose of self discovery. To 'know thyself' (*gnōthi seauton*) is as important today as it was in Ancient Greek times.

Object from nature release

This can be used with any of the letting go techniques outlined in this book or just when something comes up that you want to release, be it a person, a trauma, a job, or even a bad habit.

Go out into nature with the intention to find an object that represents the person or issue you are releasing. Open sacred space and walk around with this intention softly in your mind, *allowing* the object to come to you. It could be anything, from a stick, broken root, rock, fruit, nut, to a piece of trash or a dropped item of clothing. If it is a particularly unpleasant person or event you are letting go of, then the object may look ugly to you, possibly twisted, gnarled, dirty, rotten, or jagged. Trust your intuition. You will know when the right object is found. However do not take anything that is living, such as cutting off a branch or pulling up a flower. The object will be dead (from a biological point of view) and of little or no monetary value.

When you have your object, take it in your hands and blow all the negative emotion and energy into it - all of the imagery and feelings around the person or issue. Take your time over this and really feel into it. If tears come, let them. Keep hold of the object during any releasing. Rub it on the parts of your body where, or if, you feel energy is stuck; the belly, heart and throat being the most common areas. Visualise the unwanted energy being pulled out of you. See the object as a magnet for all the negative emotions and feelings around the person or situation.

Once you feel this is completed you may decide you want to work more deeply with the object, maybe trying the *transmuting trauma* or *clearing blocks using breathwork* exercises outlined in the the coming pages, or you may wish to dispose of the object immediately, signifying that you are finished with the person or issue and any hold they, or it, may have had upon you.

To dispose of the object, literally throw it away. Throw it away somewhere in nature, making sure it will not be found easily, by you or another, and do so with the intention of releasing the person or issue. Throw it with your full force, with a shout or angry expletive, and feel done with it. You're getting rid of something that no longer serves you, something that you may have been carrying in your psyche consciously, or sub-consciously, for a while. Do not throw it at someone, over the fence into a neighbour's garden, or in a place where people congregate. Throw it into the sea, a lake or river, a quarry, wooded area, the undergrowth, wasteland, etc., or even a public rubbish bin. Once thrown, turn away and leave the area, feeling lighter. Don't look back.

Ensure you feel grounded, any energetic gaps left by the release are filled with something positive (a warm feeling of self love, for example) and close sacred space.

Cutting the ties

Cutting the ties can be used to energetically sever the connection between you and another person, whatever their relationship to you, however briefly you knew them, and whenever they were in your life. We are connected to the people in our lives in various ways, be it genetically, emotionally, or spiritually. The strength and effect of this connection depends on the relationship we had, or are having, with the other person. For example, often when a romantic relationship has ended there remains a tie to the other person, especially if it is not a completely mutually agreed split. This can trigger repeated emotions and feelings long after the relationship is over. *Cutting the ties* is a process to finalise the split and allow both parties to move on freely.

Cutting the ties can also be part of the letting go process around any negative people, toxic relationships, even traumatic encounters, or to cut the energetic link between you and someone in spirit, a past life, a negative habit, or a situation you wish to be free from. Below are two methods that can be tried either together or separately.

For this first method of *cutting the ties* you will need a stick about 30cms (12 inches) in length. Find a comfortable and private space and centre yourself. Open the space. Visualise the person or situation you are releasing in front of you, to heighten the energy around the release. Begin by pulling out imaginary threads from your belly button. Try to really feel these energetic attachments to the person or situation you are working with coming out of you. Visualise them as unwanted energy, maybe even see them as a black or a colour of decay. Visualise yourself gripping these threads in one hand, pulling them out and cutting them away with the stick in the other hand. See the stick as a sword, knife or light beam slicing down through the imaginary threads. Bring the handful of cut threads to your mouth and blow them away, out of the window or into nature, visualising the strands disintegrating and dispersing into the ether. Keep repeating this process until you feel you have pulled out all you can and there is no more attachment left. Then place your hands over your belly button and visualise a soothing healing colour or light coming from your hands and filling your belly, replacing all that has been let go of with something beautiful and energetically nourishing. Do this until you feel balanced. Close the space, making sure you feel grounded.

The second method of *cutting the ties*, perhaps more suited to relationship attachments, is to use an imagined energy field around you, separating you from the other person. Once you have opened space visualise a force field, bubble or aura around yourself. Then see the person you wish to release coming close to the edge of it, holding out a box. This box contains everything from your relationship with the other person; physical objects, emotions and feelings. See the other person offer this box to you, allowing it to cross your boundary so that you may take it from them in your outstretched arms. By taking this box you are energetically taking back all that is yours. Feel this. Whatever your feelings may be towards the person, calmly say to them, "thank you", and "goodbye". In your mind watch them turn and walk away, walk away from your life. Really feel like you are letting them go.

Hold the box up above your head, seeing it burst into flames and disintegrating into ashes, or transmuting into sparkling light to be carried away into the ether. Let go of all of the box's contents, especially if there is an object that they have held onto such as jewellery, a book, artwork, a car, or even a house, that you feel is yours. The division and disbursement of larger items should have been agreed beforehand, possibly legally, so now is the time to let all of the objects go and move on. Allow the bubble to dissipate and return to the ordinary world feeling lighter. Close the space, ensuring you are grounded, when you feel you have finished.

Transmuting trauma

As a compliment to the *object from nature release* and *cutting the ties* exercises the *transmuting trauma* process can be used to work directly with the main issues of your life. From the list you created in the *Life CV* exercise identify the top three traumas, issues or situations you want to let go of. Acknowledging and confronting these traumas takes courage and by letting go I mean transmuting the emotions into energies that can be dissipated. The memory will still be there but the emotional charge associated with it should be eliminated, or reduced considerably. Afterwards, albeit perhaps slowly, the memory will also begin to fade. These three traumas and the people involved are the ones that you feel have had the most profound effect on you physically, emotionally and psychologically.

As in the *object from nature release*, find a natural object that represents the first, or biggest issue/person you want to work with. Keep hold of this item when carrying out the stages below. This process has its roots in the Hawaiian process called *Ho'opono pono* (which translates as 'to make right'), but this is a far more simplified version.

Firstly, find a safe and private space to work in, ensuring you will not be interrupted, preferably sat at a table. It may be useful to have some background music or drumming playing.

Open sacred space. Take some relaxing breaths, close your eyes and imagine the person sat opposite you. Wear a blindfold if that helps. If it is an issue with no others involved then create a clear mental picture of the situation as you remember it and put that across the table from you. Alternatively imagine yourself as you were during the incident and visualise that version of you sat across the table.

Out loud, say to the person/situation;

> *I'm sorry.*
> *Please forgive me.*
> *Thank you.*
> *I love you.*

Do this slowly, concentrating upon and feeling each sentence.

- *I'm sorry.* Feel repentance even if you know you were not at fault. Take a responsibility for what happened. Somewhere guilt sits between you and the other person. Maybe you are clearing for both of you. If it is a situation let any remorse take over you. Really feel this. Let any tears flow or sobbing come forth. Even curl up on the floor if that's where the pain sends you. This is your time to release. Do whatever it takes to let it out from your body. Often tapping the throat, heart or belly will help the release.

- *Please forgive me.* This shows humility. Again even if you are convinced it was not your fault, take responsibility. Take the higher ground. And again most definitely feel this. Forgiveness clears the past. You are also asking for forgiveness for yourself at the time. Spiritually we are children. We are allowed and meant to make mistakes, they help us grow.

- *Thank you.* Be in deep gratitude. For the person, for the situation that has helped you grow, for the lessons learnt, for being you, and for being able to take this step.

- *I love you.* Say this to the person or the issue and send as much love as you can out into the Universe. Realise that by saying this you are saying that you love yourself too. Accept this love back for yourself.

If you can 'see' the other person and notice how they react (in your mind) when you say and feel each of the above sentences, this may also be helpful.

You may want to repeat this process, to try and go deeper into it, realising this is not absolving anyone or anything from blame, but rather a process to help you let go of the trauma emotionally. Even if you know you are totally innocent of any wrongdoing, if you were 100% the victim, you can take this higher perspective and forgive from a place of love. This also takes bravery and courage, which reinforces your commitment to, and love for, yourself. In her book, *The Power Within You Now!*[6], Sue Stone says:

> *"The process is to forgive yourself, thank yourself and send yourself love. By doing this you erase the impact of the memory. As the suffering vanishes from within you, it also disappears from the other person or the situation."*

When you feel you are finished it is time to carry out the *object from nature release* process, as previously described, with the natural object you have been holding. Blow into it any residual emotions and rub it over your body, visualising any remaining negative energies being *drawn out* and absorbed by it, before throwing away the object somewhere where it will not be easily found.

Do this for each of the people/issues you want to release energetically. When you feel you have finished spend some time in gratitude for what you have just accomplished. If you feel drained or tired, visualise healing energy being drawn in to fill up any gaps left by the releasing, placing your hands where you feel they are needed to help direct this healing energy or light. Close space and make sure you feel grounded again before carrying on with your day.

---

[6] Sue Stone, *The Power Within You Now!, 2019, self-published.*

Transmuting deeper trauma

What about events where forgiveness is seemingly impossible? For example, prolonged mental or physical torture, war crimes, murder, child abuse or rape. Is it helpful to revisit and relive the issue? How do you forgive a murderer, a torturer, or the man who raped you as a child? It will not be easy, and if such a process feels impossible try to re-frame it. You are working on this because you want to be free of the emotion and the negative side of the experience that has, and probably still is, affecting you in one way or another. In this case, perhaps a more ritualistic approach would work better rather than the previous outlined pragmatic one.

If the incident happened when you were young put your younger self across the table from you and try saying the words I'm sorry, please forgive me, thank you, I love you, as if you are apologising to your younger self for what happened. Maybe you feel you were not protected as you felt you should have been by those who were meant to love and look after you. If you cannot face picturing your attacker or abuser as you remember them, try visualising them as a child, and see the pain they probably suffered when young that manifested in later life into the pain that they then inflicted upon you.

However, anger, hatred and thoughts of vengeance, or similar emotions are sure to surface. Are you strong enough to go beyond these, to send love to someone that has hurt you, done obscenely, abhorrently wrong by you? To perhaps break a cycle of pain that you are victim of?

This is moving to a biblical sense of forgiving sin and absolving all inflicted pain, taking tremendous courage and bravery to face and work with. I suggest that if you have been through such a trauma and can work through the process, whether you feel healed or not, then you have been truly courageous and can be very proud of making the effort. Even a seemingly minor move in the right direction is progress, and often we do not realise the enormity of our perceived small steps and the echoes they have on our soul.

Again I must point out that there is help and counselling available from trained professionals who have experience with such devastating traumas, and if you have not already, then please seek out such beneficial help with your issue. The work I am sharing here should be looked at as complimentary to any professional counselling (or similar), and I hope offers additional ways one can work on oneself to transmute emotional trauma and move forward.

Clearing blocks using breathwork
Note: Safety warning

This exercise is based upon a breathing exercise described by Wim Hof, the Dutch extreme athlete, teacher and health guru. Ensure you are medically able to carry this out as there is some strain on the heart and lungs. Do this exercise on an empty stomach and lying down in a quiet space, ideally after some yoga or light exercise to bring you into your body. You may find it beneficial to wear a blindfold or similar. As always, open sacred space.

Begin by taking a couple of breaths to relax you into the process. Then when you are ready take a full breath in, raising your belly first, then the chest. When you have inhaled fully let the breath go naturally, not forcing it out or trying to empty the lungs totally. Then begin another deep full breath in, expanding the belly and lungs to take in as much air as possible. Again release naturally. Continue by repeating this cycle; full inhale, natural exhale. You may feel tingles in your hands or your lips, and possibly feel a little light headed as you proceed. This is OK, but if it becomes overpowering stop. Once you have reached about twenty or thirty cycles, stop and hold your breath for as long as possible, without straining. When you feel the need to take a breath do so, then have a couple more calming normal breaths. This is one round.

Begin a second round of breathing and notice if there is any emotion coming up, any blockage in the body that wants clearing. If there is focus on this area as you breathe. Tapping the area where you feel the block (normally the throat, heart or belly) can lead to a release, maybe in the form of tears, a shaking, or even a convulsive guttural sobbing. Often imagery will appear too, maybe just popping into your head. This might relate to a past trauma, a fear, a person, a situation, or something else. Something that is associated with the blockage, something that needs clearing. Stay in this space to see if you want to release more, if something else comes up, or you wish to go through another round. Normally only one or two rounds are needed.

You have taken yourself to the edge with the breath and consequently, also beyond the ego mind, thus lowering the ego's defences and allowing the release. You took yourself to a vulnerable place where the mind is in less control. Fill the void left by what has been released with something beautiful - a healing colour, feeling, sound, or image, or the energy of a loved one, a guru, master or deity. Whatever feels right for you. Nature abhors a vacuum so it is always best to replace what was let go of with something positive. However being in gratitude afterwards is often enough.

When finished breathe normally and allow yourself to come back into your body and feel grounded before continuing your day. Close space. The grounding exercise described in an earlier section may be needed if you still feel floaty half an hour or more after finishing this exercise.

Taking oneself to the extreme, physically or mentally, has been, and still is, used by many as part of their faith or spiritual practice, be it breathwork, fasting, immersion in darkness, spending extended periods in silence, chanting, dancing, fire walking, or arduous pilgrimage. All push you to the limit, can drain you emotionally, and loosen the ego control allowing space for connection to something bigger.

Three perspectives

This is a simple but surprisingly effective exercise to work with releasing the emotions and energy around a negative experience in your life, one that maybe you have kept hidden or are embarrassed about. You will need a mirror you can sit and face if doing this on your own.

Open space. Begin by reliving the experience, speaking to yourself in the mirror and giving air to the emotions around it. Speak about how it made you feel at the time and how you feel now. Talk to anyone involved as if they were there in the mirror. Go as deeply into the feelings as possible, allowing any emotions to be released. When finished give yourself a moment to journal anything pertinent.

The second round is to retell your story but this time only from the perspective of what you have learnt. Share with yourself in the mirror the lessons taken from the situation or person. What insight has come from it? How has it made you stronger? If there is a person involved tell them what they have taught you whilst looking into the mirror. Again journal anything pertinent.

Finally, talk through your story with comedy, seeing the lighter side of the whole situation. Turn any tragedy, heartache, or pain into something uplifting and light. Make it into something humorous. By the end of this cycle of three ways of sharing the same story, three ways of telling it to yourself in the mirror, you should feel lighter and less burdened by any emotions. This is a good example of re-framing, to look at an issue from different perspectives. Spend a moment in gratitude and journal as you see fit.

Alternatively you could do this with friends or family members you trust. If they feel comfortable with the process maybe they can share too, but make sure everyone understands that this is not about getting help or seeking advice. It is about being a silent witness for each other. This may be difficult for others to do, not only being a silent witness, but having to hear what you say, as there might be guilt or shame if they feel they are somehow involved or connected to the issue. It may however just bring up sympathetic feelings within them as it is human nature to empathise, and sharing in a group can be very powerful.

Letter writing

Letter writing is helpful with shedding light upon emotions around a situation or a particular person, and to begin shifting these feelings. It can be especially useful if you are someone that spends a lot of time in their mind. Some obvious examples are letters to parents, guardians, grandparents, your younger self, an ex-partner, an abuser, an ancestor in spirit, God, Goddess or the Universe, but in truth you can write a letter to anyone or anything.

When writing the letter around an issue or situation, explain how you felt when it happened, what effect it had on your life, how you feel now, and how you wish to feel in the future, including what you want to let go of emotionally, physically or spiritually. If you are writing to a person then write to them directly, whether they are alive or have passed. Again write about how they made you feel at the time, any effect their actions or words have had on your life, and how you wish to feel in the future. Write from the heart. This letter should not be kept as you would be holding onto the emotions rather than working to let them go. The letter should be dispatched, either by posting or burning it. If you post it I strongly advise not to send it to the person directly but leave the front of the envelope blank so it will never be delivered, and do not put an address in the letter itself, or surnames of the people involved, ensuring the letter cannot be traced to either them or you. Give a small prayer and offer thanks when you actually post the letter, sending it on its way with love, feeling any negative emotions attached to it being taken away.

If that sounds too daunting then perhaps the next option to burn the letter is better. If you choose to burn the letter begin by opening space. Then read the letter back to yourself, ideally aloud, feeling the emotion that the letter was written with once again, and add any more words and prayers that you deem fitting, before offering it to the fire. If a real fire is not possible then lighting the letter with a candle and dropping it into a fireproof dish to burn is fine. Try to do this outside so that the smoke can be taken away on the wind, along with your prayers for transformation and forgiveness that the letter represents. Again, and as always with any spiritual work, be in a space of gratitude afterwards and close the space when finished.

For a more physical approach you can hold your own ceremony of release. If it is based around grief for the loss of a loved one then this ceremony can take the form of memorial service that you can conduct yourself. See *The West* chapter for how to conduct such a ceremony.

A letter can be burnt, an object can be blown into and thrown away, a ceremony can be held where words, emotions and energy are offered up to Great Spirit, God, the Universe, or whatever is beyond our consciousness. These are all actions of giving away, of releasing and letting go. Anything that is in alignment with this letting go process will work in a similar way, helping to release the negative energy around a person or situation.

Releasing with water
Note: Safety warning

Working with water holds an inherent danger, especially if you go out of your depth, are not a strong swimmer or are working in fast flowing currents, powerful waves or strong tides. Please be safe when attempting any of the below exercises.

Negativity wash off

Use water to help wash away unwanted or negative energies, or help let go of people, places or events from the past. Use the action of the waves, the current of a river or stream, or maybe the pounding of a waterfall, to wash away this negativity. Ideally you should do this exercise physically - on the beach, in the sea, in a river, a lake, or under a waterfall - but of course, your location and the weather may make this difficult. If being in such a location is not possible then make use of your bath or shower, a hot tub or swimming pool, or just visualise the scenario in your mind during meditation. As always, open space before beginning. There are various options to work with the flow of water as outlined below.

If on a beach then stand ankle deep in the waves facing out to sea. Let all that you need to let go of fall from your head and body, down and out of your feet to be taken away by the waves. Visualise the outgoing waves carrying off this negativity into the vast ocean in front of you. When comfortable with this proceed to visualise positive energy flowing into you with the incoming waves, energising you from your feet and up throughout your whole body. Play with this cycle of ebb and flow. As you sink into the sand feel you connection to the earth grow. Keep your balance and ensure you don't get stuck!

Similarly, if you are lucky enough to be on a warm beach, try laying down in the tidal zone, so the lap-water can reach your whole body, without completely covering you face and affecting your breathing. Close your eyes and allow the gentle action of the waves to wash away any unwanted energies. Visualise whatever needs to be let go of flowing out from you, as a colour, a feeling, or an emotion, and being taken away by the gentle caress of the waves. Allow this energy to be released and washed away into the vast ocean. Again with the incoming water fill yourself up with a positive feeling or energy. Through these cycles of ebb and flow feel connected to both the earth below you and the water flowing over your body. Embrace this process as a physical and emotional cleanse.

A similar exercise can be carried out in still water, such as a lake, pond or swimming pool. It is useful to use a floating device for this exercise, ideally a swimming noodle. Find a comfortable position floating on your back. Then close your eyes and tilt your head back to submerge it, leaving only your nostrils above the water. With your face just under the surface breathe calmly through your nose. Take time to get comfortable with this unusual position, under the water but still able to breathe. Feel the weight of the water on your face. Relax into this and let whatever you are releasing dissolve into the water as you calmly breathe. When you surface, do so slowly, and feel the water drain from your eye sockets and face, washing away further unwanted energy and leaving you in a relaxed state. Repeat and play with this.

This exercise can also be tried in the bath, but will require some physical manoeuvring, probably with your knees up to give room to immerse your torso. If you do not have good upper body strength this could be a difficult position to get back out of, so please be cautious if attempting this.

When working with flowing water, such as a stream or river, make sure it is not too deep before stepping into the flow. You may need to wear boots or waders if the water is cold. Find your balance and stand still, allowing the water the flow around your feet. Become comfortable in this position, adjusting your balance as necessary. Visualise the current drawing out and taking away whatever it is you are releasing, seeing negativity draining from your body, going down to your feet and out into the flow of water. Visualise it dissolving and being carried away downstream. Similarly feel the water flowing into you from upstream, bringing in positive energy and filling you up feet first, replacing what is being let go of.

If you can visit a waterfall and the water is warm enough then this is a similar process, albeit somewhat more energetic. Firstly, getting yourself near the waterfall will take some effort and, depending on the volume of water flowing, you may not be able to get underneath it. However you can get close and float nearby, listening to the thunderous roar and visualise your energetic body being purged and cleansed. Again a similar exercise can be played with in the shower at home, using the cascade of water to wash away what is being let go of. If there is room try sitting down under the shower and work with the flow of water from here. As this is not the usual position adopted in the shower the mind can focus more on the intention, improving the effectiveness of the process.

Alternatively you can use visualisation to imagine yourself in nature, in the stream, the river, the sea, a lake, on a beach, under a waterfall, etc., and maybe visualise the water not just as water, but maybe a ribbon of light or a beautiful cleansing energy. Simply allow the flow to wash over you, taking away what needs to be released and replacing it with something positive, something nourishing and uplifting. At the end of the exercise give thanks and close space.

Sensory play like this, activates and stimulates nerves, thus mimicking a feeling of release, of negativity being washed away. The scientific mind will say that this is all that is happening. A nerve activation, a physical sensation. But when married with visualisation this sensory play can create a powerful emotional response well worth exploring.

Gratitude stones

Gratitude is a cornerstone of any spiritual and shamanic work. Once the work has been carried out, the exercise completed or the ceremony over, then we should always take time to give thanks.

Take a walk in nature, in your your garden if you have one, and find two small smooth stones. These can be used as your gratitude stones. Hold one in each hand, bringing the stone in the right hand over your heart, close your eyes, and give thanks for your life and anything you are feeling grateful for that day. Whatever comes to mind for you is fine. Repeat this every day. The stones will *grow* with this gratitude energy. Keep them on your spiritual altar or even by your bedside as a reminder.

Some areas for gratitude are:

- Your home and neighbourhood.
- Your family and friends.
- Your job and career.

- Your health. It is often something we take for granted, especially when we are young. In later life, as problems may occur, health can become a number one priority.

- Fresh air and water. Again taken for granted for the vast majority of people in the western world but as industry and pollutants have infiltrated our lives, clean air and water are not always guaranteed, especially in the more impoverished areas.

- Your food. Give thanks before eating, saying a blessing or prayer showing gratitude for the journey your food has taken to your plate and the sacrifice made by the natural world so that you can eat.

- You. What are you thankful for about yourself? Focus on what you like and love about yourself. Self love and treating yourself with gentleness, can foster internal harmony.

Letting go of possessions

We all have objects, photos, or keepsakes, that we feel we must never part with, or that have a potent emotional charge associated with them. Normally they remind us of a departed loved one, or family member, a special period in our life, or a particularly memorable moment. These memories are clearly ours and can never be taken away, but memories can fade. There is also something special about holding an object, holding something that you know someone else held, or gave to you with love. It represents a connection to someone or something in your past and carries with it an emotional energy. This is true in the spiritual and shamanic world, as objects from nature can be used to hold and transmute energies, just as in the *object from nature release* exercise.

So why not for all objects? Indeed religious relics are deemed priceless by devotees of that religion, such as the Shroud of Turin in the Cathedral of Saint John the Baptist, Italy, or the Beard of Muhammad in the Topkapi Palace Museum, Turkey, Buddha's tooth in the Temple of the Tooth, Sri Lanka, or the numerous encased saintly remains (normally bone or hair) locked away in churches and cathedrals around the globe. These relics are venerated by the faithful and have taken on an almost supernatural mystical power.

Heirlooms of course have sentimental and often financial value. To give away such items would seem on the surface to be difficult for a number of reasons. It may feel disrespectful to the family, or to the memory of the person who gave it to you and, from a financial perspective, it could be deemed wasteful, squandering what was bequeathed to you. This does, however, highlight the attachment we place on possessions, and not just heirlooms, but many everyday items such as favourite clothes, a well worn pair of comfy shoes, a cherished car, or a house full of memories. In fact anything can be an origin of attachment. This is the western way, and certainly true in the UK. Letting go of this attachment and letting the item go from our lives, may ultimately be freeing, but often difficult to do in practice.

So firstly begin by having a clear-out. Part with all that can easily be let go of and is of little monetary value. Then progress to those items that fall into a *keeping just in case* category. Is it really likely you will need it? Could you get something similar if you ever do need it in the future? Then look at unused or rarely used items. Could they be given to charity? Look upon your gift as a way of passing on any joy the item gave you to somebody else. Apportion a financial value if you wish and think of your donation as a monetary figure that you are giving to charity. Finally move onto items of value that are purely for decoration or are keepsakes. Which ones can you give away? Maybe give them to a family member, a friend or to charity.

What items can you absolutely not give away? List them down and make a note of the emotions that come up when thinking about actually giving each away. What is stopping you from letting these things go? Is it the memory of a loved one? A crossroad moment in your life? Do you feel you do not have the right to give it away? Is there a seemingly unbreakable promise around an item? There could be many reasons. Going deeper into these reasons can add more information to your *Life CV* from earlier in this *South* section.

Perhaps keep all your heirlooms together in an ancestor box (see *the North* section). If you feel brave enough then give away / pass on these items of sentimental and financial value. How do you feel afterwards? Lighter, regretful or a combination of emotions? Whatever the objects were, trust that they have gone to someone who will enjoy them or make use of them. You are in effect *paying it forward*.

Handover ceremony

If you have an object you cannot let go of try holding a handover ceremony. Firstly be clear on the reason why you cannot let the object go. Then find an object in nature, a natural item that you are drawn to, that can represent this precious object you are struggling to part with. You will also need a length of colourful ribbon, cloth, or similar.

The intention is to instil the energy of one into the other. To do this put both objects side by side on your altar, touching if possible, wrapping the ribbon or cloth around them, connecting them physically. Speak out loud your intention to swap the energies and state any other thoughts or emotions around this handover, such as why you are struggling to let go. Leave these objects on your altar for a few days or until you feel comfortable that an energetic exchange has happened. Now you have two objects that represent the same thing. Is it now easier to give a way your *precious* object? In the future, if the time comes, it should also be easier to let go of the object from nature, whatever it represents.

For example, if your mother has sadly passed away and the only piece of her jewellery you have is her broach, the thought of giving it away seems impossible. So you go looking for an object in nature and are drawn to an acorn for some reason. Placing these two together on your altar, cupped together on a beautiful purple satin cloth, you look at and hold them both each day, remembering your mother fondly. When holding them you speak out loud to your mother in spirit, speaking your truth, releasing any emotions, sometimes almost chatting with her.

After a week of this you feel it is time to let your mother's broach pass to someone else, so you take it to your favourite charity shop, saying goodbye to it one last time. However each day afterwards you still look at and pick up the acorn and realise that the connection and love is till there, within this acorn. As time passes the acorn on your altar gets lost but you don't mind, as every autumn there is an abundance of acorns to act as a reminder of your beloved mother. In fact whenever you see an acorn, outdoors, in a magazine, or on the TV you are reminded of your mother and a smile comes to your face.

Apologies to any mums that don't like the thought of being compared to or replaced by an acorn, so maybe a sea shell, poplar tree, or even a garden bird, say a robin, is a better object of remembrance. Something that reminds you of your mother whenever you see or hear it.

Illness and disease

Letting go exercises are not only useful when working with past traumas or emotions but can be used if suffering from an illness and disease. Begin by visualising the illness then use one of the letting go processes described above to transmute it and visualise it leaving your body. For example, see cancerous cells as dark blobs that can be washed away by water in one of the using water exercises, or a tumour be broken apart when energetically pulled out by an object from nature.

You could also try the transmuting trauma and *Ho'opono pono* exercises, visualising the disease as a mass sat opposite you at the table, as there may be emotion or trauma associated with the illness that may only become apparent when working with it. Try writing a letter to the problem or talking to the illness whilst in meditation or journeying. Is it trying to tell you something? What are you not listening to in your body?

Other methods to work with ill health are to visualise yourself healthy using rebuilding metaphors; maybe see yourself as a castle that has a few holes in the walls that need filling, or as a jigsaw with a couple of wrong or missing pieces. Rebuild your castle. Complete your jigsaw. Additionally you could visualise healing actions taking place within you, such as seeing broken bones knit themselves together, just as a weave of woollen threads, or just visualise healthy cells multiply, crowd out and vanquish (or eat up) any diseased ones.

Talk yourself better, by being positive and telling your body it is healed, and include an uplifting statement of fact about having a healthy body in any affirmations you work with, but be wary of washing over any deep emotions by superficially covering yourself in a comfort blanket of positive thinking, or false optimism.

For pain relief try visualising the area as being calmed from an angry red to a peaceful blue or green, or the flame of pain being doused by a stream of water. See an intense pain as being like a tightened vice that you can ease off before seeing it fall away completely, or a clamped claw that you visualise releasing, maybe even watching the creature it belongs to fly away. Find a metaphor that works with you and the pain you feel.

After any healing work around letting go or the removal of the unwanted, visualise yourself bathed in a healing light or colour, or a spiritual or divine energy, to fill any energetic gaps created by the release, sending love to those parts of you that need it.

The West - Facing fears and death

"I could get right by myself. I could make it right, if i was brave enough, to listen to what was in my heart and do something about it."
Bhodi Rook, Rogue One.

The West section looks at facing your fears, feelings around death, and living your life as well as you can. It is represented by Jaguar (female) in the symbolism this book draws upon. A powerful animal stalking us through life, able to strike at any time from the shadows, but also a mother and protector, teaching us to bravely face life head on. The exercises in this section can help answer some penetrating questions; What fears do you have? What fears have been inherited? What are your experiences around death and losing a loved one? What are your feelings about your own mortality? What are you doing to really live your life now? Are you living healthily? Are you honouring the sacredness of the life you have been given?

Move out of your comfort zone

Something we haven't tried before, or haven't experienced does not have to loom large over us and create fear. Even if we have trepidation with an activity, it is unlikely to be as bad as we think it will be. Spending time out of your comfort zone can help dissolve fears of the new, the unfamiliar and the unknown. There are clearly various ways this can be done but a few simple ideas are:

- Vary your walk to work or when running errands. Take another route even if it may be longer.

- Visit somewhere new.

- Talk to a stranger. Do this each day for three days.

- Wear clothes or a colour you wouldn't normally.

- Try different foods.

- Change the way you automatically do something. For example, washing your hair, taking a bath, making a meal. Try doing it differently, even if it feels slower or less effective.

- Try a new pastime or activity.

- Challenge yourself. When you hear yourself give advice or an opinion, challenge yourself. Are you sure about what you said? Why did you feel the need to say it? Is there another perspective that you may not be seeing?

- Individual space. Personal boundaries are developed so that individuals feel comfortable when interacting with others. Social limits and cultural differences affect these distances, as do medical situations; e.g., social distancing during the coronavirus pandemic. Try blurring these lines a little, allowing others to come closer if they wish (as long as it is safe). Understand why you do not (or maybe do) like people coming closer.

Fears
Note: Safety warning

There are a variety of ways to approach fears and understand any anxieties around them. The idea is not to overcome the fear, although that may be desired if it is affecting your life detrimentally, but to embrace it and, as the saying goes, "feel the fear and do it anyway". The chemical rush, the buzz of adrenaline, is palpable and searched out by many to add to the spice of life, such as watching horror movies, clambering through pitch black cave systems, or jumping out of a plane at 12,000 ft.

Beyond any obvious traumatic experience that could have left scars and an inherent fear, there are other areas to revisit that may have had a detrimental influence on you, quite often rooted somewhere in childhood, such as:

- Being lost (e.g., in a crowd, shopping mall, or forest)
- A fear inherited or *picked up* from a parent.
- Being bullied (by a sibling, by someone at school, by a child/adolescent living near you)
- Unsafe (in retrospect) situations around, for example, water, heights, confined spaces, crowds, loud noises, certain people.
- An unwelcome encounter with a wild animal, perhaps being startled by it.
- Scared by something you were told, read, watched on TV or saw on the internet.

In fact any negative experience in your life could be a root cause of a phobia, and it is worth adding any profound fear from this list to your *Life CV* from *The South* section, estimating if necessary when it first started or became apparent.

The most effective way to treat a chronic phobia is exposure therapy, whereby the individual is assisted by an experienced therapist to approach the object or situation that they fear, while being coached on how to deal with their anxiety. This can be done very gradually, over a number of sessions, or in a single prolonged session, depending on the individual's readiness to progress. Fear of animals such as spiders, rats, pigeons, snakes, dogs and insects are common animal phobias and ones that can be controlled and overcome with such exposure therapy, but there are also actions you can take for yourself. Firstly ask yourself some questions or meditate around the issue. Can you recall when this first began? Is there a reason or a root cause? Was there an incident with this animal in your childhood for example? Read a book about the animal, ideally one with pictures. Understand as much as you can about the animal, its evolution, natural behaviour and its place in nature. Make note of any remarkable or positive characteristics. Then move on to more tactile interaction. Paint or draw the animal, keep a photo of one with you and become familiar with it. Buy yourself a toy of the animal and watch documentaries about it. Visit a pet shop or zoo to *meet* the animal. Take measures to become comfortable being near one in captivity.

All the above should help alleviate fears around the animal but you can also carry out a shamanic style journey to the spirit of the animal to unearth more information as to why you feel the way you do about it. Maybe there is a hidden message from the animal for you, some wisdom that you need to learn or incorporate into your life. See the section on shamanic journeying for more information on how to do this. If you are unsure of a spirit animal's meaning to you, search for it on the internet and see if the information given resonates.

For other types of fear try testing yourself in small, totally safe ways. For example, if your fear is heights then look at activities such as going up the stairs in a tall building and looking out at each floor noting how you feel. Or push a little further by trying to walk across a high bridge, zip lining or canopy walking. If it is confined spaces try spending time in small spaces that you can easily leave such as a shed, tiny room, or cupboard. For darkness wear a blindfold for a period of time. Again carry out a shamanic journey to uncover any deeper meaning to your fear, perhaps seeing what that fear represents metaphorically in your journey. Is it a person or situation from your living memory, or maybe a past life manifesting in this life? How can you make peace with this fear? Perhaps one of the *letting go* exercises from the previous section would be helpful when dealing with a fear and it's root cause. Of course, if you feel your fear or phobia is affecting your day to day life then obtaining professional help is highly recommended.

There are a number of other methods to go deeper into fear and challenge yourself on a more general level, such as wearing flamboyant clothing that draws attention, speaking in public, singing in a choir, volunteering where you will come into contact with others, or even going as far as trying a firewalk.

Shadowself

We all have a shadowself. That part of us where our faults, inhibitions and fears reside. Our own personal demons. We all have them, as nobody is perfect. Nor should they be for that matter. Life is not about being perfect or striving for perfection, be it in physical appearance, home and family life, relationships or achievements. Whomever you may know or read about in a magazine, seen on TV or the internet and think they are perfect or have the perfect life, rest assured, they have their own issues and troubles going on one way or another. The key is to not let your perceived negative reactions and behaviours control or define you. Accept you have a shadowself. Own it. Realise that it may come out now and again, and may seem to control your actions at times, but also accept that it is there for your own benefit and growth as a person.

Try listening to the script in your head. What keeps repeating? What negative judgements do you have about people you know? What do you not like about them? Is there a trace of the trait within you? Life is often a mirror so when we moan about someone or something, our feelings are actually coming from a similar place within us. As the saying goes, "It takes one to know one." We can also expect too much from people, especially if we expect a lot from ourselves (maybe as a result of demanding or exacting parents), and if such expectations are not met then the result can be a sense of lack or failure. Are your expectations of other people's behaviour, and your own, too high? Where in your life are you setting standards so high that failure is almost guaranteed?

List down your perceived negative traits, characteristics and behaviours. In the UK we find it quite easy to see the negative within ourselves rather than positive, so don't be surprised at a long list if you are British! Against each negative trait write down the opposite. Against this positive characteristic list out the times in your life when you have shown this. When completed this list details the negative characteristics you believe you have, with their opposite positive characteristics, both of which you have felt and expressed. Hopefully this should show you that you are a far nicer, a far better person, than perhaps you thought you were.

The shadowself is a teacher. It has served you in the past, often as a way of protecting you. Your *loyal soldier*, as I heard it once said, fighting your corner. Do you still need him or her fighting so strongly for you? Try asking your *loyal soldier* to step back. Meditate or journey with it, thanking it for all the protection it has given you over your life, but now it is time for it to take a back seat.

Antagonist list

In a similar way to the shadowself exercise, think of a person from your life, who you believe has affected you detrimentally, and list down the negative traits you feel they possess or that they showed you, one below the other. Then across from each one write the opposite positive trait. Do you think they have any of these good characteristics? Why did you see the negative? What do you think is stopping them from being the positive? Do you have any of these negative traits? The answers to these questions may show you that the judgements made about others may not be as clear cut as first thought. Maybe they are reflecting back to you part of yourself, revealing more of your shadowself.

Mistakes

We have all made mistakes. They are part of learning, of growing up, and come with the territory when trying something new, stepping outside of our comfort zone, or when we are working from a place of not knowing. Therefore, most of the time, we can can let them slide, especially if we feel we have learnt any inherent lesson. However there may be some mistakes, made recently or in the past, that still carry some guilt or shame, and an act of atonement felt necessary. If you feel you have made such a mistake, for example, by wronging someone, letting someone down, or not behaving as you think you should have, then try one of the letting go exercises covered in the previous section. Alternatively make a note of the pertinent mistakes and then jot down alongside each one the lesson hidden within.

Maybe hold a ceremony to apologise to anyone you may have hurt, giving thanks for the lessons and letting go of any emotion attached.

A simple ceremony is fine, lighting a candle, writing and burning a letter, using an object from nature, or a simple prayer sat at your altar. Take responsibility for your actions, even if you think others were at fault or to blame. Owning the situation is different from accepting all the blame yourself. By working on and releasing any negative energies around the event, you not only help yourself, but in the global landscape of energetic interaction, you may be helping any others involved, even if the *how* is unclear to you.

Making mistakes in spiritual work is fine too. Again nobody is perfect. If you feel that you may have done something incorrectly or been disrespectful, then stop, apologise in your mind or out loud and carry on. We are all children spiritually. All mistakes are forgivable, as there is not one spirit, ascended master, benevolent ancestral force, god or deity that would not forgive a child, especially if that child was trying to learn and grow.

Darkness

Darkness is where we come from, within the womb, without light. But it holds a primordial fear. As children, darkness can be the place where monsters await, the bogeyman's domain, the doorway to nightmares. It represents the unknown and a place where fear lurks. As we grow up hopefully this fear of darkness passes, or is at least diminished, but it is easy to see why such a fear perpetuates. In reality darkness accounts for a third of our lives, the time we are sleeping, and is not something to be afraid of.

Of course, nightmares do occur, conjuring up something in our imagination we perhaps do not want to face, reliving a dreadful experience, or a general manifestation of our fears. Life anxieties too can lead to restless sleep and long nights. All this makes bedtime, night time and darkness a place that can hold fear for us. It is, however, the mind chatter that create the fears and uneasiness, not the darkness. So it worth befriending this blackness, for darkness should be welcomed as a friend and not feared as a foe.

Darkness has been used by shaman, mystics and similar seekers for centuries, millennia even, as a place of refuge, a place of peace and a place to explore and to find insight. There is an inherent stillness in darkness, made more acute by the fact that we cannot see anything within the blackness. This lack of visual input forces us to make use of our other senses, which in turn takes focus, slowing us down and moving us deeper towards stillness.

Making use of chambers within the ground, such as natural caves or a burrow physically dug out of the earth, like the ancient burial mounds found across the globe, certain types of North American sweat lodge, or the kivas of the Pueblo people, can give not only the dark space to *work* within, but also provide a deeper connection to the planet, by being held within the womb of Mother Earth if you will. Where the ground is too hard to be excavated then man made above ground structures, such as certain temples, ceremonial structures, or above ground sweat lodges, have been used for the purpose of ceremony and connection to the darkness. Finding your own cave may be quite tricky nowadays. You may be able to convert a room (a basement is ideal) in your home by blocking out all the light to become your own *cave*. However this is not practical for the majority of people, so wearing a blindfold (a Mindfold is recommended) is a good alternative.

Purposefully spending time in darkness can have a number of benefits. Firstly it can help face any fears held around being in the dark, maybe stemming from childhood. We all had nightmares of one sort or another when we were young and they can echo throughout out adult lives. Secondly, darkness is the place to go for meditation and visualisation. Our focus is sharper and images can be more vivid. Just closing your eyes is acceptable but it is not true darkness as the eyelids are opaque, allowing some ambient light in, especially during the daytime. Wearing a blindfold will allow total darkness to be worked with. This also alleviates light from any automatic eye flutter and, if a Mindfold is used (which has cut outs for the eyes), allows the wearer to stay in total darkness even with eyes relaxed or half open. Thirdly, after a period in darkness your other senses become heightened. New feelings and sensations can come up to be explored and played with. Even just the sense of entering another world. Finally, going into darkness for spiritual work is linking you directly to those that have gone before. As mentioned, many cultures have used darkness for spiritual experiences across the planet for millennia. By doing so yourself you are joining a long line of seekers and are connecting to the explorer energy that is within us all.

Even if we feel quite content in the life we have, there is always a questioning part of us (albeit possibly suppressed), that wants to know just a little bit more, go somewhere new, or try something different. Variety is, after all, the spice of life. So, even if just once for the experience, it is worth spending an extended time, whilst awake, in darkness.

Note: Safety warning
When we are in darkness others automatically know to leave us alone; "Don't disturb her, she's sleeping/meditating/praying". If you sit on a park bench with your eyes closed it is most likely you will not be disturbed. People know to leave you alone. Try it. At first you will be aware of everyone passing by you, and you may feel that they are looking at you or about to disturb you. Let this pass and slowly sink deeper into the darkness. If you do this on a sunny day

notice the *colour* of the darkness you are in. If you look towards the Sun with your eyes closed, *see* the colours as they slowly change and immerse yourself in each. Reds, oranges, yellows, maybe some indigo and purple, even flashes of colourful light. Of course, do not look directly at the Sun with open eyes, or even half open eyes. This can permanently damage your eyesight.

A final point to make, on an evolutionary note, is that before the dinosaurs there was another mass extinction event (science says there have been at least five such events in the Earth's history) that wiped out most species except for those living underground. It is highly likely our pre-dinosaur ancestors were burrowers and lived most, if not all of their lives, underground and in darkness. Perhaps our connection to the darkness is part of our genetic make-up, passed on through our DNA. I suggest working with darkness reignites this part of our chemistry and is something we have evolved to work with. If not why would the effects of working with darkness be so profound? Evolution tends to only keep what is necessary and what works.

Darkness exercises
Note: Safety warning

The below is a rough outline of an approximately two hour session and includes a number of suggestions for exercises that can done whilst in darkness. Initially, or if you have some reservations about darkness, try just immersing yourself for a few minutes to half an hour. Ideally though it is worth spending two to three hours in continual darkness.

Before beginning a long session in darkness do all you can to ensure you will not be disturbed, so that your focus will inward and without distraction. You will be moving around in darkness so familiarise yourself with the space you will be in for the period. You may stay in one room or, as is more likely, you will be moving around your home. Prepare the space by clearing the area and remove anything breakable. Gather a few objects from your altar to work with, along with something wooden (i.e. your tapping stick) and a stone or crystal to represent *Mother Earth*. Have a blanket, some water to drink and some tissues handy (as emotions may be released). Ideally also have a rattle or hand drum nearby, and prepare any music that you are going to use; you may find it beneficial to have some gentle background music or a drum beat playing throughout your time in darkness, but this is a personal choice.

Create a space where you can be lying down with everything you need within easy reach. Let's call this your ceremonial area. Firstly open space standing in the middle of your ceremonial area. Then go into darkness by putting on your blindfold. Spend some time acclimatising to the darkness and wandering around your space. Be conscious of slowing your movements down. Explore the room you are in. Touch things, get your bearings a little. Start by going a small distance and then returning to your ceremonial area. Then try going further. Be still often, just listening. If you need the bathroom try to stay in darkness whilst you use the facilities. If that is not possible spend as little time as possible out of darkness.

Whilst in your ceremonial area work in turn with each of the altar objects you have chosen. Try meditating with each or focusing upon one as you rattle or drum and carry out a journey with it. Or just hold each one in turn and move around your area, *seeing* (in your mind) or feeling what comes up. If emotions rise, allow yourself to go fully into them and releasing where necessary. Tapping parts of your body with your stick or fingers can help with the release.

Once you feel you have completed the work with the all the objects chosen from your altar take a moment to give thanks for anything that has been released. Then ensure you feel grounded again before continuing.

Try any or all of the following:

- Practice yoga or any other gentle movement routine you are familiar with.

- Use a rattle or drum and gently move, sway or dance. Be aware of the space around you, being careful not to knock anything over. If you have prepared it, play some music and dance away with total abandon, again being conscious not to fall over or crash into anything.

- Try an energy visualisation by imagining pulling in energy, as a colour, ribbon of light or similar, from above, down into your head, through your body and into the ground. Then reverse this and draw energy up from the earth, through your body and out of the crown of your head into the Universe. Play with this.

- If you are feeling adventurous maybe go outside into a garden or similar, if you have a private and safe space to do this. I strongly warn against going out onto balconies or other high places as you will be in a disorientated state and liable to trip or topple over. Also it is likely that you will be experiencing heightened feelings and the sense that you will want to fly could be quite overpowering. Do not go out into a public place or near any traffic due to the obvious dangers.

Return to your ceremonial area and again take some time to give thanks, centre and ground yourself. Go back into silence and lay down, focussing your intention towards connecting to *Mother Earth*, making sure your wooden object and stone or crystal are close by. Take hold of the wooden object and visualise yourself in a wooded area connecting to the trees, their strong trunks, the branches reaching up to the sky, the roots going down into the earth. Meditate, journey or just be with this visualisation. Spend time in this wooded area and feel welcomed by the trees, really feel your connection to them. Communicate with them and allow the dialogue to flow. What do they want to say to you? What do you want to say to them? Play with this. Then take your stone or crystal and visualise yourself going deep into the earth and connecting with the rocks, maybe in a cave deep within the earth or in the heart of a mountain. Again play with this through meditation or journeying, saying what you wish to say to the planet and hearing what the rocks, the earth and the energies deep within the planet wish to communicate with you.

With both the wooden and stone or crystal objects follow your intuition and allow your visualisation and the sensations felt to strengthen your connection to the Earth. Allow yourself to be transported throughout the natural world and visit any natural place, or meet any animal that you wish or that the darkness wants to show you. At some point ask *Mother Earth* what is her greatest need right now and what more can you do to help her? When finished give thanks to *Mother Earth*, for all that she provides, and ground yourself.

Other activities to try in darkness:

- Chant, recite a mantra or just play with sound and your voice. Maybe find your own sound, a sound that resonates with you. (See the *The North* chapter.)
- Listen to nature.
- Pray or meditate.

- Focus on your body. Touch, massage and caress yourself.

- Have a bath (safely!)

- Draw something or be creative in a simple way, using your other senses rather than sight.

- Eat something (made beforehand, easily prepared without sight, or something prepared for you.) Focus on the smell, taste and texture. Notice how your eating automatically slows down when in darkness.

Please do not try to cook, boil water, make a fire, or carry out any other potentially dangerous task.

Bring yourself back to your ceremonial area and, as a final exercise in darkness, try visualising or journeying to a cave or underground temple, and feel the presence of the ancestors in this place. It has seen a millennia of spiritual people, seekers and pilgrims immerse themselves in the darkness, connect to the planet and be given insight on their life journeys. Now you are here, exploring this liminal space. Connect to those that have gone before and spend some time in gratitude.

It is now time to say thank you to the darkness and to return to the light. Stand up in your ceremonial area and visualise roots coming out from your feet. Spend a few moments bringing grounding energy up into your body from the earth. Give thanks for your time spent in darkness and for any insights you may have been given, before gently removing the blindfold. Ensure you feel grounded and close the space. Afterwards spend some time noting how you feel, maybe journalling any experiences and insights. Are there any issues or fears that came up that were not suitably resolved? Try to be gentle with yourself for the rest of your day or evening.

Grief for a deceased loved one

"But what is grief if not love persevering."
Vision, WanderVision.

Grief is a process. It is different for each person and there should be no expectation on how one should grieve. We are however, conditioned in the west to be somewhat reserved when it comes to grief, to hold things in and not show any emotion, as we are told this is a sign of weakness, for men in particular. But this attitude is unhealthy as being aware of, and able to express our feelings, is a sign of emotional maturity and a strength, in both men and women.

Emotions however can get stuck, or be locked away, and slowly begin to fester. The more we bury them, the more impact they can have on us at a physical level. They are burdens we do not have to carry. If someone we love dies, someone we were close to, it hurts. It is painful. That person is no longer part of our daily world. No more sharing of good times, no more confiding in, no more helping or being helped, no more of their *energy* around, no more of their love to receive and, just as sadly, they are no longer there to receive our love.

But we still have our memory of them. We can imagine or visualise them. So start by doing just that. If there is someone you have lost then begin by imagining them. See them at peace. If there were unresolved issues, things left unsaid before they left, then visualise saying these things to the person. Say whatever words come to you, whatever feels right, whether you believe they can hear you or not. It is for you to shift the emotion. Creating a virtual conversation allows you to go into the emotion and release it. By releasing I mean allow yourself the space to cry, scream or curl up on the floor sobbing. Go wherever the emotion takes you. Try not to talk through any tears, or hold back. This stops the process. If you feel you need emotional support (or indeed physical) try holding onto something wooden, a staff or stick for example, to feel the connection to something natural and to the earth. If you want to help the visualising process, hold an object that belonged to your loved one, or something that reminds you of them, whilst saying what you want to say. Tapping, with your fingers or a wooden stick, on your throat, chest and belly areas may be useful as this can help shift energy.

Maybe go to a place that reminds you of them and give a (biodegradable) offering, saying some words or a prayer whilst there or write a letter to your loved one and burn or post it, being mindful not to include names or addresses. If drawn to, carry out one of the letting go exercises from *The South* section.

Use the *clearing blocks using breathwork* exercise from *The South* section if you are not able to go into the emotion as deeply as you would like, or try holding your own memorial service for your beloved. This will give you time and space to go fully into any emotion, respectfully and privately. See the next section for a general outline.

When we are with someone else that is suffering with grief, as much as we may want to, it is best not to comfort them if they are in a state of release, as this stops their grief process. We want to reach out and ease the pain they are clearly going through and, in turn, reduce the pain we are empathetically feeling. However this deprives the other person of a chance to go fully into their own process. In a public funeral situation it is of course natural to hold and comfort those grieving. It would seem inhumane not to. But in truth to go fully into the emotion it needs to be faced alone, head on, and without any shame or embarrassment.

How to conduct your own memorial service

"We've cried long enough. Let's do something that lets us love, respect and honour them without being morbid all the time."
Said in 1996 by Viola Parker, wife of Sergeant Earl Parker, killed in action over fifty years previously on D-Day 1944.[7]

In western society there is an organised funeral immediately, or relatively quickly, after the death of a loved one. However this is too soon for most people to work through their grief, especially if the death was sudden. The funeral serves a purpose of course, but the immediacy of its occurrence, the formalised ritual, any religious influence and the relatively impersonal nature of the ceremony may not feel right for truly expressing one's grief.

Holding a separate, deeply personal memorial service, or passing over ceremony, for someone you love, makes it far more applicable to you and your relationship to the person. Such a ceremony provides a space where the grief process can be entered into more fully, without your guard up or, as is often the case in the UK, with a *stiff upper lip* and keeping the emotions under check, especially in the case of men. Some people may feel they never grieved properly for a loved one. Maybe they didn't want to express their emotions at the time, did not have a chance to grieve fully for one reason or another, or felt they had to be strong for the rest of the family.

The circumstances surrounding the passing of a loved one also have a major impact on how our emotions manifest. The shock of a sudden and unexpected death, a tragedy in which a life is lost, can mean the grief process is almost bypassed and the emotions not

---

[7] From *The Bedford Boys* by Alex Kershaw, 2004, De Capo Press.

given a chance to be accessed, let alone be expressed. Of course, even the passing of someone naturally from old age can still be difficult and surrounded by grief.

Then there are global issues, such as the coronavirus pandemic that began in 2020. COVID-19 affected everyone on the planet and has taken (and continues to take) many lives, in some instances very quickly, often with the patient allowed very limited contact with family and friends towards the end of their life. Additionally, and understandably, to minimise transmission of the virus, the number of funeral attendees was restricted in the UK (as in most countries), depriving people from being able to pay their respects in person. Even if people could attend there were probably still certain COVID-19 guidelines to follow and an underlying concern about being around others in a group situation, however slim the chance of infection, thus distracting the attendees further from being fully present in the ceremony.

Other large scale losses such as disease, war, famine, genocide, ethnic and religious cleansing, natural disasters, etc., all lead to the loss of lives in devastatingly traumatic ways. All loss of life is hard to take, but when it seems senseless, of no fault of the deceased, based on circumstance, colour of skin, sexual orientation, faith or just bad luck, there is an inherent disbelief, a lack of understanding, outrage and understandable anger at what has happened, all of which overshadow and undermine the grief process of those in mourning.

For all and any of the circumstances around the loss of a loved one, conducting your own memorial service can offer great solace. There is no time frame for conducting such a memorial. It can be held relatively soon after the formal funeral or years, even decades, after your loved one has passed. The service can be either individual or with a group, but I suggest trying the individual ceremony first to familiarise yourself with the process and give yourself the opportunity to tap into your own grief, allowing the release and the expressing of any emotion. In both cases the ceremony is conducted predominately for the people present, not the deceased. By that I mean the ceremony is for you and, in the case of a group ceremony, also for those you have invited, to go fully and openly into the depth of the felt grief. It is not meant to be a celebration of the life of the deceased. This can be done at another time in another ceremony. If the deceased was religious, or if there are certain beliefs to be honoured, then by all means incorporate them in some way, but do not feel that the ceremony has to be led by these beliefs.

As individuals perhaps we do not feel qualified, or possibly feel scared, about conducting our own memorial service for a loved one, thinking that we may get it wrong or be disrespectful, especially when there is such a well established industry around such matters. There is however no reason why you cannot hold your own ceremony for a loved one in any way you see fit, but I strongly advise that it should consist of a beginning, a middle and end. Ending a ceremony is especially important psychologically, as this draws a line under proceedings and formally concludes the ceremony, thereby providing a form of closure. The below outline is a suggestion that you may wish to use. Both the individual and group memorial services follow a similar outline:

- Prepare the area ready for the ceremony.
- Open the space.
- Conduct the memorial service.
- Close the space.
- Give thanks and ensure everyone present is grounded.
- Clear the area of personal items.

As a note, conducting such a ceremony doesn't mean that you are having to let their memory go totally, or are saying goodbye forever, let alone be free of all of the emotion or feelings you have for your loved one. The pain may well endure, the grief still be present, but it is my hope, and experience, that you will be lighter and more comfortable in your own feelings, knowing that you have held a sacred ceremony based upon the love you had for the deceased. Of course, you're loved one will not be forgotten and forever live on in your memory.

Individual ceremony

The ceremony described here has its roots in the natural world and my shamanic training. As far as I know it is not an appropriated sacred ceremony. As every culture and society has their own take on how to prepare a loved one for whatever lies beyond this life, there is no right or wrong way to carry out such a ceremony. There is also no need for any religious or spiritual beliefs to conduct such a ceremony. Intention, respect and love are all that really matter.

Plan and prepare for your ceremony. Pick a time and day, and choose a suitable space to conduct the ceremony, ideally a private space and one where you feel comfortable releasing any emotion, either indoors or outdoors is fine. The dress code is entirely up to you. Dress up if you like, wear black, or be casual. Whatever you feel comfortable wearing is OK. Collect together a few of your loved one's personal items, such as clothing, shoes, jewellery, etc., along with one photograph. The following may seem a little macabre but I suggest positioning their possessions as if the deceased was laying down. Use a rolled up blanket, pillows or cushions, covered with a sheet or similar to represent the body and adorn it with their clothes. Place shoes at one end, jewellery where it would normally be worn and put the photograph near the head area. An actual photograph or one on a phone or tablet is fine. If you do not have any personal items, just lay a sheet over the rolled up blanket, pillows or cushions, and place a surrogate pair of shoes one end and the photograph at the other. There's no need to go into too much detail here, just enough to evoke the sense that their body is in the room. Don't forget a glass of water and a box of tissues. It's worth preparing for some emotion to come up, and in doing so, you are subconsciously telling yourself that shedding tears is OK. In fact during this preparation process you will probably be feeling very emotional anyway. Go into the emotion as it comes up. Cry. Release. You don't have to *save up* the emotion for the ceremony itself. This whole process is for you to go as fully as possible into your grief, allowing emotion to come up and be released, whenever and however it manifests. In a way, this process started as soon as you decided to conduct a ceremony.

Before you begin the ceremony open sacred space. You should be familiar with opening space from the previous exercises but I shall reiterate the process here as a reminder. Opening space marks the beginning of the service, recognising the space as being ceremonial (for the duration of the ceremony), and is a way to say, "I am here and I am ready to hold this ceremony for my loved one." However you wish to open space is fine as it is the intention that counts. Some suggestions are to either say an opening prayer, invite the spirit of your loved one to be present, call to the directions (north, south, east, west, below and above), connect with God, Goddess, religious or spiritual leaders, angels, spirit animals, or ask for ancestors and other loved ones in spirit to come and be with you.

There is no right or wrong here, or a necessity for any belief in the afterlife to do this. It is the intention that holds the power, not the reality of the situation. The intention is to offer an invitation to those unseen (and energies unseen) to be present with you at this ceremony and comes only from a place of love.

You are asking for help in shifting the emotions of this life, the powerful emotion of the loss and passing over of a loved one. It should feel both respectful and comforting. At no time should there be a fear of ghosts or anything supernatural. Only ever love. Alternatively, just offer up a humble request to the Universe or for that which is outside of your consciousness (maybe just your subconscious), to be present with you today for this ceremony. Allow any wording to come from the heart. As it is the intention that matters, however the words come out will be fine. If you are unsure prepare something to say beforehand and have it ready on a sheet of paper. Even though you are conducting this ceremony by yourself, try to say any words out loud and not just in your head. Burn some incense, smudge (the wafting of smoke from smouldering sacred plants or wood), or light a candle if you are drawn to. Play background music if you wish. Create an atmosphere that feels right for you.

So you have prepared the space, set the scene and asked for help from whatever lies outside of your consciousness. Now is the time for the main body of the ceremony and for you to speak from the heart about your loved one. In fact, speak your words as if they can hear you. Say what you want to say to them. Maybe say things that were not said when they were alive. Clear the air, get everything off your chest. Speak as if you were having a conversation with them, with their spirit. By pretending they are there, or they are listening, whether you believe they can hear or not, psychologically brings you closer to them, or to the memory of them, thus creating a more personal and authentic ceremony. This in turn can make for a deeper release. Talk freely with them, chat about whatever comes up. Even seemingly banal things if they come to mind. There is no need to rush so spend as long as you want with this. Accept it will be a one way conversation but be open to signs of a response, an acknowledgement from the Universe for your humble ceremony. Maybe seeing a certain bird or animal in your garden, hearing a specific noise from outside, or even seeing a particular image or programme on TV or the internet later that day. Do not get caught up in a two way dialogue unless you are comfortable with your psychic abilities.

If at any time you feel like you want to cry, sob, wail or collapse, do so. This is the time, and an ideal chance for such a release of emotion; a clearing of any emotional blockage. Feelings of embarrassment may surface by this show of emotion, but as you are conducting the ceremony alone and in private where nobody else can see or hear you, these feelings should pass quickly. Be brave. Go as deep as you can. Tap the throat, heart or belly areas with your fingertips or a short wooden stick to aid the release. You can also try drumming or rattling (a steady medium paced beat) to give a background pulse to help occupy your mind and drive the release. If you don't have a hand drum or rattle there are audio files or videos online that can be used instead. Having a wooden staff or walking stick for support and grounding is also useful as it is something natural to hold, giving a strong connection to the earth.

Many emotions can come up, and perhaps not only around the person you are holding the ceremony for. Others who have died may come to mind, as may a pet or beloved animal, and you may release emotion around their passing. There may even be emotions around wider issues such as the coronavirus pandemic, habitat loss, species loss, pollution, disease, war, famine, natural disasters, etc. Allow whatever that wants to come up to be expressed and released.

When you feel you have released as much as possible, tell your loved one that it is time to send them on their way. At this point you may want to drum or rattle, and visualise their spirit being taken away into the ether. Maybe chant or sing, and say "goodbye", "thank you", "I love you", or any other parting words you wish, words to help send them on their journey beyond this life. There is no right or wrong here. If it comes from the heart then it is right. Feel as though you are helping them on their way, letting them go to wherever and whatever lies beyond.

This intention of sending them on their way reinforces any similar soul flight that may have occurred since their death. Even if you (or the deceased) have no belief in an afterlife, speaking out loud helps shift the emotions, more so than just thinking the sentiment. The act of sending them on their way as best you can is a potent symbol of your love. It can often provide some level of closure. As a suggestion try using a bird of prey, maybe an eagle, in your visualisation of their spirit or soul moving on. Visualise the eagle coming down and lifting your loved one up and away into the sky, reuniting them with the Universe/God/Great Spirit. Do your best to set them free and let them go a little more in your heart.

When you feel ready, just as you opened space at the beginning, at the end of the ceremony close the space. As a reminder, this is done simply by thanking those unseen that you invited when you opened the space, for coming and being present with you throughout the ceremony, whether you felt their presence or not. If you called in the directions, turn to face each one and give thanks. Give a final thank you to your loved one, knowing that you have done your best in sending them on their way spiritually. Spend a few moments in gratitude for what has transpired and feel proud that you have just completed a beautiful ceremony honouring your beloved.

Afterwards ensure you feel grounded and back in the present moment. As a reminder, a simple way to do this is to imagine roots coming out from the bottom of your feet into the earth and connecting you to the planet. Feel balanced. If you have one, hold a wooden staff or stick, and feel the direct connection down through the wood into the earth. Alternatively having something to eat or drink, or going for a walk in nature are good ways to ground yourself.

As soon as possible after the ceremony and when you feel able to, clear up the area where you have been conducting the ceremony, removing all the items. Try and do this with a lighter heart and with a feeling of gratitude. It is difficult to let go of a loved one's treasured belongings but try to keep only a few items. Be careful not to create a shrine as this is *holding on* rather than *letting go*.

If, on reflection, you feel there was more to be said, or you feel that you didn't do something correctly, you can always try writing a heartfelt letter to the deceased and posting it to the Universe or burning it ceremonially. Alternatively, hold another memorial service at a later date. However if the intention was there, then one ceremony should be enough, even if it was not exactly how you wanted it. Undoubtedly it was as it should have been.

Group ceremony

If you wish to hold a memorial service with other people I strongly advise conducting one on your own first, to familiarise yourself with the process and provide the opportunity to tap into your own grief. Invite those you wish to attend and inform them a little of the process, asking them to bring one object that reminds them of the deceased. Also advise them on what to wear. People often default to black, but whatever people feel comfortable wearing to such an event should be fine. However you are holding the ceremony so whatever feels right needs to be communicated.

On the day of the service prepare the space where you are going to conduct the ceremony, using the rolled up blanket or similar to represent the body and place the objects and photograph appropriately. Keep one particular object for the ceremony itself. Have water and tissues handy. When all your guests have arrived make them as comfortable as possible with what is about to happen. When it comes to conducting a ceremony, it is hard to please everyone due to the variety of beliefs, but it is the intention and an open heart that matters. Let them know this is a safe and loving space to show and release their emotions.

Open the space as you choose to. The same method as used in the individual ceremony is fine. Smudge or burn incense and light a candle. Play some background music, but remember this is not a celebration of the life. This is a ceremony to provide a space for those present to release, to let go and move through the grief process. So the music should be soft, soothing, maybe even sad. This is a space to go into the sadness, into the grief, and release it, not to mask or avoid it. As with the individual ceremony, invite God, Great Spirit, ancestors, the directions, etc., to be present. Whatever feels right for the group is fine, even if it is just calling to the Universe.

Start the process yourself, thereby showing the others what to do, by placing the object you have kept back on the representation of the body, and speaking your words to your beloved. Talk from the heart. Then invite each person in turn to come to the body, place down the object they have brought and to say what they have to say, speaking as if the deceased was in the room. Give everyone time to say as much as they wish and allow them the space to release. I suggest that if anyone does begin crying, sobbing or wailing, or even if they collapse on the floor, allow them the space to do this without consolation.

It is only natural that we want to console someone who is grieving and clearly in emotional pain. We want their pain to stop. We don't like how their pain is making us feel as it holds up a mirror to the grief we may be struggling to release from our own hearts. But by going to them, by holding them or comforting them, only acts to interrupt and stop their grief process. If you feel you must do something, tell them they are being very brave and now is the time to go deeply into the grief. Often one person's courage to lay bare their emotions can be a trigger for others present to do the same. One person's crying gives another permission to cry. So expressing these emotions is both cathartic and helpful to the group. Only if deep emotional releasing is prolonged and becomes too much should anyone be helped and comforted. You have to be the judge of this. Drumming or rattling with a repetitive beat can be used to distract people's minds and help with grounding during and after the sharing and release.

Once all present have had their time to speak, give everyone a final chance to say something. Often by being in the ceremonial energy and witnessing family members open up, others can become confident to speak freely from the heart.

Conclude the ceremony by singing or chanting, sending the energy or spirit of the deceased on their way and saying goodbye. Keep any chant or song simple, short and repetitive, so that all present can join in easily. Ideally do not to use words, as these convey a certain meaning and not everyone's interpretation will be the same. Try singing or chanting from the heart and see what notes come out. As with the individual ceremony ask those present to visualise the spirit of the deceased being taken away to the heavens, maybe by an eagle, to be reunited with the Universe, the ancestors, Great Spirit or God.

Allow the energies of the ceremony to settle, maybe with a few seconds of quiet contemplation.

Give thanks to those present for coming, for being open to what has just happened and to feel proud for being part of a beautiful ceremony honouring a loved one. Close the space and thank those unseen, be they ancestors, Great Spirit, God or the Universe for being with you today. Encourage everyone to ground themselves, imagining roots coming out of their feet and going deep in to the earth whilst taking a few balancing deep breaths.

Clear the space and remove all the items and possessions as the ceremony is now over. Do not leave the objects in place to become a shrine. Giving away your loved ones personal objects, perhaps saving only a few keepsakes, is cathartic and can be done when the time feels right. Love is about letting go, not holding on.

It is a good idea once the ceremony is formally closed to share some food and drink, gather around a real fire, or go for a walk together, so that everyone can share, relax and feel more grounded.

The loss of a baby or child

Losing a child is painful whatever the circumstances and the grief felt is certainly unimaginable to those that have not been through such a traumatic event. Some comfort may be found in conducting an individual memorial or passing over ceremony, in a similar way to that outlined above. Of course there are likely to be a wider range of emotions felt, such as a deeper sense of injustice, a more pronounced feeling of loss, tremendous guilt (whatever the circumstances of the death), acrimonious blame, the shattering thought of a life not lived, a potential not even begun to be fulfilled, and the opportunity to raise a child to adulthood and pass on wisdom and knowledge taken away. It is also not the normal order of things. A child should outlive their parents.

I would suggest that any memorial is carried out with both parents present instead of individually, as this allows for each parent to be there for one another and to understand more of the others perspective, as the mother and father may differ in their grief and how they show it. Then, if wanted, a larger ceremony can be undertaken with more family members. To represent the child use something small (maybe a doll or teddy bear) wrapped in a blanket. Again use a photo and place any sentimental objects on or near the blanket. Carry out the memorial in a similar way to that outlined previously, again with the primary intention to work through the grief from such a tragic loss.

The loss of a child through abortion or miscarriage is clearly also traumatic, particularly for the mother, who may have had to face such a loss in private, possibly even alone. There is no reason why a memorial service cannot be held for this loss. Carry it out in a similar way to the loss of a child ceremony using a small doll/teddy (or whatever feels right for you) wrapped in a blanket to represent the unborn life. Also I suggest not giving a name to the child if it was never met in life. Often a name may come to the parents once a child is born, a different name from what they imagined or decided upon beforehand. This is, however, a personal choice.

Gravestones, memorials and the scattering of ashes

The use of a gravestone, memorial plaque, planting of a tree or any other way of remembering and honouring your loved one, are all personal and entirely up to the individual and family wishes. However, I would say that it is best to avoid forming a shrine to the deceased. This is often the case when it comes to the loss of a baby or child. Many small graves in cemeteries are elaborately decorated and adorned with children's toys, playthings and often many photographs. Clearly any comfort that can be taken by the parents and family by tending the grave is what is most important, but be careful not to let it become a shrine over time. How much time is enough is up to the individual, and each parent or family will be different, especially when there is peer or family pressure, guilt, or shame.

To let someone go (whatever their age) with love is to set them free. Holding their memory in your heart is enough. Conducting a memorial service or passing over ceremony as outlined above may help with this. Scattering ashes is clearly personal and can be carried out any way you see fit. By all means create a ceremony around the process, but saying a few words, or even just being in a loving state of remembrance when you scatter the ashes, is enough to honour your beloved.

The after life

Currently, from a scientific point of view, nobody can confirm or deny the existence of an afterlife, although psychics, mediums and many spiritual or religious people are convinced of it. It is worth being open minded because, as with many unknowns, perhaps one day the scientific community will be able to observe, measure and explain certain spiritual phenomena, giving credence to long held beliefs of something beyond this life. That day may be a year, twenty or five hundred from now, so in the meantime we have to rely on our own experiences and intuition, and decide for ourselves.

Something to be aware of is that many people have reported similar experiences towards the end of their lives, such as in the case of near death experiences (NDEs). Dr Penny Sartori, was awarded a PhD for her research into NDEs in 2005, based on seventeen years working as an intensive care nurse in the UK, and has written a number of books on the subject. The below extract from an article by Brian McIver for the Daily Record[8] explains more:

> "Over a four year period Dr Sartori spoke to patients who had actually died, after a cardiac arrest where their heart stopped beating. She found out that seventeen percent had a NDE.
>
> *'They are all unique, but they do tend to follow a pattern. Some report travelling through a tunnel towards the light, and feeling magnetically drawn to the light. Once in the light, they find a beautiful landscape with lush green grass and beautiful flowers.*
>
> *They often meet deceased relatives, and sometimes a being of light or religious figure, who are usually associated with the person's own religion or culture. Very often, they have a conversation with the relatives or the being of light, who tells them to go back, it's not their time. Others will have a life review, where they will watch their whole life pass before their eyes, or have an out-of-body experience, where they view their own emergency situation from above.'*

---

[8] Brian McIver, article *Ex-nurse Dr Penny Sartori studies amazing experiences of people who come back from the dead*, Daily Record, 25/01/11.

In the thirteen years Dr Sartori has been studying NDEs, she has heard some incredible accounts.

'One man had a very clear out-of body experience, which I had published in a journal. He very accurately described my and the doctor's actions caring for him, at the time he was deeply unconscious. He gave a very accurate account of what had happened, and also described going into a pink room, where his dead mother and a Jesus type figure told him it wasn't his time and he had to go back. He was sixty and had suffered all his life from cerebral palsy. From birth, his right hand was in a contracted position but, following his experience, he was able to open up his hand. There was no medical explanation for that at all. There are other cases where people have been healed, but all we know is there is something going on that we can't explain.

When I started, everyone thought it was a bit of a joke and made fun of me. But as it progressed and more research came out, more people started to take notice and doctors are becoming more open-minded and more aware of it. The most important part is the idea of consciousness, where it begins and where it ends. These experiences have given us different ideas of what we currently believe consciousness to be, so we have to keep an open mind, and a lot more research is needed. I am a lot more open-minded. We need to do a lot more research and look at things differently. Science says consciousness is created by the brain, but maybe is just mediated by the brain. Through studying death, what it has really taught me is more about life, and how precious it is.'"

Dying impeccably

Death and the thought of death are somewhat taboo subjects in many modern western cultures even though we know we are all going to die. The fears around death can be diminished if one takes time to focus upon it and, to some extent, prepare for it. If your time was up, if a giant asteroid was going to hit the Earth tomorrow annihilating everything, what regrets would you have about your life and how you lived it? What would you want to do with your last 24 hours alive? What has previously stopped you doing these things? Has anything been left unsaid or unresolved? Who do you need to forgive? Who do you need to apologise to? If it is difficult or impossible to speak to these people try writing them a letter and either positing it to the Universe or ceremonially burning it.

Bronnie Ware is an Australian nurse who spent several years working in palliative care, caring for patients in the last twelve weeks of their lives. She recorded their dying epiphanies and put her observations into a book, *The Top Five Regrets of the Dying*[9], summarised below:

> "1. *I wish I'd had the courage to live a life true to myself, not the life others expected of me.*
> This was the most common regret of all. When people realise that their life is almost over and look back clearly on it, it is easy to see how many dreams have gone unfulfilled. Most people had not honoured even a half of their dreams and had to die knowing that it was due to choices they had made, or not made. Health brings a freedom very few realise, until they no longer have it.

---

[9] Bronnie Ware, *The Top Five Regrets of the Dying, 2012, Hay House.*

2. *I wish I hadn't worked so hard.*
This came from every male patient that I nursed. They missed their children's youth and their partner's companionship. Women also spoke of this regret, but as most were from an older generation, many of the female patients had not been breadwinners. All of the men I nursed deeply regretted spending so much of their lives on the treadmill of a work existence.

3. *I wish I'd had the courage to express my feelings.*
Many people suppressed their feelings in order to keep peace with others. As a result, they settled for a mediocre existence and never became who they were truly capable of becoming. Many developed illnesses relating to the bitterness and resentment they carried as a result.

4. *I wish I had stayed in touch with my friends.*
Often they would not truly realise the full benefits of old friends until their dying weeks and it was not always possible to track them down. Many had become so caught up in their own lives that they had let golden friendships slip by over the years. There were many deep regrets about not giving friendships the time and effort that they deserved. Everyone misses their friends when they are dying.

5. *I wish that I had let myself be happier.*
This is a surprisingly common one. Many did not realise until the end that happiness is a choice. They had stayed stuck in old patterns and habits. The so-called 'comfort' of familiarity overflowed into their emotions, as well as their physical lives. Fear of change had them pretending to others, and to themselves, that they were content, when deep within, they longed to laugh properly and have silliness in their life again."

Death is inevitable and therefore worth planning for and certainly worth talking about. In many cultures death and the passing of a loved one is ritualised and celebrated with ceremony and festival. The day of the dead in Mexico is an annual festival that honours the deceased, and a time when families gather and pay their respects in remembrance and celebration, rather than in sadness and regret.

Whilst travelling many years ago I visited the area called Tana Toraja, on the island of Sulawesi, Indonesia, and came across a festival in full flow, with music, food and drink, and rodeo like activities happening in a central arena. Myself, and the friends I was travelling with, stopped and inquired as to the reason for this gathering, and were told this was another day in a six month long funeral of one of the local community elders who had passed a number of years ago. The family had spent the interim years saving up enough money to afford such a festival, so that their loved one could be sent on their way in the fashion their status demanded in the Toraja culture.

Such cultures, where death is an accepted part of life, diffuse the fear around it, as it is something the community are familiar with. This familiarity is made all the more poignant when it is the family and local community that deal with the deceased and the funeral itself. In the UK we defer to others when it comes to the final moments of life and our subsequent passing. Towards the end we are told what to do by strange doctors and nurses, hospital or hospice staff then, after our passing, our body is handed over to another set of strangers for cremation or burial, and often with a relatively impersonal ceremony.

An open casket wake may seem macabre to our standoffish point of view but there are a number of benefits that can help diminish the stigma around death. Firstly it gives the opportunity for those that attend to see a dead body, perhaps for the first time in their lives, thus building up a familiarity with death. Secondly, this is a chance to see a loved one at peace and (normally) in their own home, where we knew them to be happy and content, rather than the last place they were alive, be it a hospital or hospice bed, both impersonal places of suffering. Finally it offers a chance to say goodbye to the deceased, perhaps in a similar way as described earlier in the section *How to conduct your own memorial service for a loved one*.

A final point on dying is having the ability to be able to control your death. This really is about planning for your passing, ensuring your affairs are in order, any regrets or unsaid words are dealt with, any funeral arrangements planned and provided for, those around you know your wishes, procedures or systems are in place to help with any foreseeable problems with your passing, and you have enough pain relief, clothing and equipment available so that you will be as comfortable as possible towards the end. Any medical professionals or spiritual counsellors should be aligned with your wishes and ensure that you are made aware of anything that may happen to you including physical changes and possible symptoms or side effects of medication. Such planning and foresight is one thing if we are facing a long term illness but the occurrence of a sudden or swift passing must also be taken into account. We never know when our time is up so it is prudent to take some time out to face our own mortality and become a little more familiar with the ending of our lives.

Living impeccably

If we are going to think about dying impeccably then surely we should consciously try to live impeccably. This may seem like a high ideal but it does not mean being perfect. It means honouring and being true to yourself, your emotions and feelings, and caring for your mind and body. Taking steps to look at all areas of your life from a healthy lifestyle perspective is worthwhile, remembering though to be gentle on yourself and make changes gradually. Most people are aware of the effect their lifestyle can have, not only on their physical body but also on their levels of energy, stress response and general well being. Exercise, good sleep patterns, positive relationships, social activities and taking time for oneself are all known to have benefits.

One of the biggest impacts on our health is the food we consume. Dietary choices are clearly important, with the effect the gut microbiome has upon overall health becoming more and more accepted as a key factor. A good varied diet to nourish the human body and the non-human microbes, especially those in the gut, and can help the fight against illness by boosting the immune system and other bodily defence systems. Although in its infancy the ability for diet to eradicate or fight cancer is showing promising results. Affecting the bacterial flora of the gut microbiome is a personalised science though. Each person's gut is different so development of a dietary plan has to be tailored to the individual. A particular food item, even if labelled a super food does not necessarily mean it will be helpful for all those who eat it.

Additionally, our diet is very different from that of our ancestors, especially since the advent of large scale farming and processed foods. The increased use of fertilisers, pesticides and chemicals, married with the use of preservatives and artificial flavourings in production, have changed the food we eat beyond what our grandparents would recognise, let alone what those cultures that live directly off the land would know as food. Pollutants too have found their way into the food chain, and are now being ingested by us. This all means our diet and the food we eat is as important to our health and mental wellbeing as any other facet of our lives.

Living impeccably also calls upon us to find ways to live as richly and harmoniously as possibly, to pursue happiness, but not at the sake of all other aspects of life. Philosophy, both ancient and modern, points us towards a considered life, to contemplate upon and engage with life. This will be discussed further in *The Centre* chapter.

The North - Seeing the magic and joy in life, and connecting with the ancestors

*"It has taken an eternity to make us yet
our life spans are brief."*
Buddhist monk.

The North is represented by Hummingbird and is the direction in which we honour those that have gone before, and realise that wonder, magic and joy are a part of life, even if at times we lose sight of this. The hummingbird is a magical creature. How can she fly as she does? The speed of her wing beat, her aerodynamics and manoeuvrability. She puts on an aeronautical display, flitting from flower to flower in her search for nectar, moving forwards, backwards and sideways at will. This shows us that metaphorically we do not always have to be moving in the same direction to be making headway on our life path. Hummingbird's diminutive size masks the ferocity with which she defends her territory and nest. Small does not mean weak. Determination, doggedness and courage are attributes hummingbird reflects back to us. How determined are we to achieve what we want in our lives? What is our epic journey? We have much to be thankful for and, whatever our upbringing, we have survived and are at the forefront of human evolution. Our ancestors had different opinions, beliefs and behaviours. Their world and culture was different to ours, but there are similarities. What can we learn from them? What do we need to remember?

From this point on I will not keep mentioning the opening and closing of sacred space, or ensuring you feel grounded after an exercise, as this should now be fully ingrained.

Paths to happiness

There are many simple actions you can take to boost your happiness, such as:

- Smile
- Foster relationships
- Move and dance
- Laugh or watch comedy
- Be active
- Meditate
- Listen to music
- Give yourself a treat
- Recall past positive experiences
- Perform acts of kindness
- Clean something
- Repair something
- Cook a wholesome meal
- Practice mindfulness
- Express gratitude
- Practice forgiveness
- Create purpose in your life
- Be creative
- Go outside and be in nature
- Stroke a pet or friendly animal
- Caress yourself.

Connection and the senses

We are in a constant state of connection. Firstly, our biology and physiology connects us genetically to our ancestors and, if we go back far enough, to the last universal common ancestor (estimated to be 3.5 billion years ago), and subsequently to all life on this planet. That is quite a link and one that can easily be dismissed, especially when we look at the diversity of life on Earth.

We are also connected to the world around us, connected to it by our senses, giving us instant feedback as to the environment we are in and how we are experiencing it. Remove one of the senses and we immediately feel a partial loss of connection but over time this can be overcome by a subsequent increase in sensitivity of one or more of the remaining senses, as the brain rewires synapses to compensate. Daniel Kish, President of World Access for the Blind, is a completely blind man from California who *sees* the world by using vocal clicks as a form of echo location. His hearing, and the parts of his brain used to process sound, have been adapted to allow him to interpret his reflected clicks as a mental map of the environment. He describes the world in front of him as composed of textures, rather than the visual description a normally sighted person would give, and is quite skilled and comfortable navigating in this way.

In a physically impaired situation, such as Daniel's, this compensation by the brain and the other senses happens automatically, but it can also be experienced to some degree if you artificially remove one of your senses, e.g., wear a blindfold for an extended period of time. There will be a noticeable change in your other senses, and perhaps the realisation that the world can be perceived in a different way, as highlighted in the darkness exercises from *The West* chapter.

Tuning into the senses, giving each one a little more focus now and again, can help with our connection to the world and our place within it, especially if we are harbouring feelings of separation. Strengthening our connection improves our feeling of belonging, and this, in turn, can aid mental health. Belonging to something, being part of a group, a member of the team, being a supporter, a follower, a disciple or worshipper, all reinforce this sense of belonging. Ultimately this can evoke within us a feeling of *home*. Not in a bricks and mortar way, but rather as a sense inside that we are where we belong, in a place of connection and shared values. If you go out into nature and actively sense and cultivate this connection to all that is around you; to the plants, trees, animals, stones, mountains, rivers, oceans, clouds, wind, rain, Sun, Moon and stars, you will be tapping into the same feelings, the same emotions and deep set awe that many, both today and throughout history, have tapped into; this sense of belonging and connection, and our intrinsic ability to feel the energy of life. One is never alone in nature.

Conversely a city life can wear these connections down, even cut them, leading to a loss (some would say a soul loss) to a degree; losing the part of you that is not used, diminished or disconnected. Fortunately, even though this can feel like a loss, it can always be reversed, brought back and reinstalled, simply by spending time in nature.

The senses and how to work with them is a vast subject with countless books, courses and therapies devoted to each. Importantly, the senses work together, so while one may seem dominant the others still have a role to play. The obvious example is food, where it is not only taste that is important to our eating experience, but also how the food looks, its smell, texture, even the sounds made as we chew. A few ideas are touched upon here, but if you are drawn to one in particular then try to explore it as deeply as you can.

Sight - e.g., light, darkness, colours, shapes, mandalas, art, the natural world, imagery created in the mind, colour therapy.

Actively seek out nature to interact with and gaze upon. Even if you are in a city try wandering in a park or around your neighbourhood absorbing the sights, as well as the sounds and smells, perhaps filtering the man made from the natural. What reactions to you feel? Do you honour that internal calling to nature or mindfully overcome it on a daily basis? Meditate whilst softly gazing at a beautiful flower (an African violet is one of my favourites).

Sound - e.g., vibration, resonance, sounds of nature, drumming, music, singing, cymatics (the geometric patterns sound creates in liquids), chanting, tinnitus, sound healing, ASMR[10], silence.

Sounds are used to great effect on TV and in movies, e.g. In the movie Star Wars the robotic droid R2D2 does not speak English, instead communicates with electronic chirps and beeps, from which it is easy to understand the context of what it is trying to say. A couple more good examples of sounds exactly communicating a feeling, this time from TV, are Pingu's squeaks and squawks, and the Teletubbies' gibberish. Of course these programmes are aimed at children but as all parents know, when communicating with an infant or toddler non linguistic sounds are natural.

Notice the sounds around you? How noisy is the place where you are? how many are natural sounds? How many man-made? Which sounds are peaceful to you?

---

[10] ASMR - Autonomous sensory meridian response, or the tingle you get in your brain or down your spine triggered by soft sounds such as whispering, the crackling of food cooking or even gift wrapping!

Touch - e.g., textures, intimacy, connection, sensual healing, massage, numbness.
Feel the objects in nature as you pass them; touch the bark of a tree, hold a stick or a conker in you hand, caress the grass, reeds or leaves of trees as you walk in nature, feel the heat of the Sun, stroke a pet animal.

Taste - e.g., food joy, unsafe food identification, saliva generation (to start the digestion process).
Taste your food, savour every mouthful. Allow your taste buds to come alive and sense the sweetness, sourness, bitterness, saltiness, or savouriness. Be open to trying new foods and going to new places to seek them out.

Smell - e.g., pheromones, smudging, cleansing, warning of fire, spoilt food, breath, air quality, ripeness, essential oils, perfumes, aromatherapy.
What smells take you away instantly, often to childhood? What smells calm you? Do any energise or excite you? Do you find any supposedly normal smells nauseating? Conversely are there some smells you like that most other people are revolted by?

Clearly each of the five senses could be expanded upon as they are whole subjects on their own, but let's delve a little deeper with sight, specifically colour, and sound.

Sound

The use of sound and vibrations in engineering is continually being explored and developed, from using standing waves to suspend objects in thin air, to an MRI guided ultrasound that can be targeted to raise the temperature of cancerous cells above fifty-five degrees and kill them. Under development too is a sonic fire extinguisher for helping with the increasing problem of wildfires around the globe. A small hand held version has been shown to put out a fire with a pulse of bass sound, generating a vibrating air column that deprives the fire of oxygen and extinguishes it. Vibrations on a larger scale, as those generated by earthquakes, can wobble or even bring down buildings at certain resonant frequencies.

Energy at the right frequency can become highly potent. Perhaps there are certain frequencies within our vocal range that are beneficial to us and can be used for relaxation, energising ourselves or even healing. For centuries certain tones or chants have been used to tap into such phenomena, especially in the Eastern mystical traditions.

Toning and chanting

The repetitive nature of a chant can be very relaxing, as cycles of breathing in and chanting out, married with the physical vibrations produced by the sound of the chant, induce a calming effect. The sound can be combined with such visualisations as breaking up energetic blocks, supporting our immune system or attacking an illness within us.

Find a sound you are drawn to, one that resonates within you. Use it as your own form of directional ultrasound. Just as ultrasound is used to break up kidney stones for example, use your own sound to break up emotional blockages, relax tensions or destroy diseased cells. Visualise the negative energy being diminished, being eradicated, and carried away by the sound into the ether. If you cannot find your own sound use the universal chant *Om*. Use the whole of your mouth and throat to create the chant. Vary it and see how the tone resonates in different areas of your throat and head. Play with this and chant with varying tones, volumes and mouth positions, noting any energetic shifts.

Find your sound

Following on from the above try finding your own sound by creating different noises vocally. Play with the sounds you can make. Vary everything. Change the pitch and volume, the position of the tongue or lips, flex the throat and vocal chords. Change the breath, breathing from the belly or chest. Open and close your mouth, hum, or even mouth a scream. Let out a full scream if you are comfortable to do so, or into a pillow so as not to disturb others. Move the whole of your face as you make the sounds, screwing it up and stretching it out. Avoid using groups of words or meaningful sentences, as they are often clumsy in describing the feeling or emotion they are meant to impart. Poets and songsmiths have wrestled with this throughout history. Use single syllable words, such as *love, peace* or *Om* and play with their sound. Finally, find sounds that resonate with you for certain scenarios. They may be different from ones suggested in books or the internet. Find your own sound to help with relaxation and calmness (i.e., a long nasal tone), anger (throaty), letting go (deep and guttural), joy (high pitched), and so on. Try finding your sound as part of the extended time in darkness exercise from *The West* chapter.

Music

Are singers and bands just entertainers? For sure, they give us music that we enjoy, want to sing or dance to, but they also impart something else. Music can provide a framework for healing to take place, as good a framework as provided by any shaman, priest or healer, for example. Musicians effortlessly and whole heartedly play and sing for us to feel emotion and heal, if we so wish. In their own way they drum out a beat for healing.

Music can evoke powerful emotions within us and, like many of the arts, can reflect back to us our mood, influence our outlook and provide an outlet or even an escape from our day to day lives. The emotional power of music is clearly illustrated in the use of film scores. Remove the music and the vast majority, if not all movies will be greatly diminished in their artistic value. For example, the film scores of John Williams have rightly won numerous awards, enhancing the vision and power of the movies he has worked upon, beyond anything the director and actors could solely produce. In fact composers, as do probably most musicians, know of tools, techniques, and sonic tricks that can be utilised to increase the impact of their music, and create a soundscape that represents and expresses the feelings and emotions they are wishing to convey. Such techniques include using call and response, repeated themes, harmony and dissonance, and the symbiotic relationship between major and minor keys, all of which, when incorporated correctly, can take us on an emotional musical journey.

Every country, every culture has their traditions, and wisdom to pass down through the generations, often in musical form. This, in turn, influences the younger generation and the direction of the music of that nation. The range of music is vast but sometimes, as a musician matures, there is a draw to folk music, the music of the people. A music that can transcend pop culture and often contains similar messages in the varying folk traditions around the world. Commonly messages of freedom, love and understanding, capturing in the words and music a connection to the past.

Freedom tunes

What are your freedom tunes? Which songs, or pieces of music, make you want to soar? Which fill you with love? Conversely which tunes make you want to weep, scream, curl up in a ball, or perhaps take you to a point of despair? Songs are powerful and take us to places, to people and back to emotionally charged events. Often there is only a short period where music is a big factor in our lives, namely when we are young, and it is from this repertoire of songs that we often listen to in later life. Hence it is quite normal for older people to be unaware of the current music scene and prefer their music, or music from a particular era, that they formed an emotional attachment to when younger. Remember though that new songs will one day be the next generation's favourite tunes and freedom songs, so never be quick to judge how bad the current music scene may seem to you. There is always wonderful new music if you are open to it, perhaps with more abrupt or cutting language but, as with all music, it is a reflection of the times, and a heart felt attempt to share the emotional landscape the musician is exploring.

Create your own freedom songs playlist and add to it as and when you hear or remember another song that moves you in any way. Take time choosing your songs and putting together your playlist, enjoying the process but also allowing any emotions to come up and be released as you go through your musical collection. With the advent of the internet it is now possible to discover and download almost any song in recording history, so if one pops into your mind that you do not own, a simple search should offer a listenable and downloadable result.

You can use this playlist in ceremonial work (see below) and allow it to take you to various emotional places or just put it on when you are in the mood for some good music. Ensure you include the upbeat songs alongside the more melancholy or sad ones, so that when you listen to the playlist you can be taken through a whole gamut of emotions.

Five songs

From your freedom tunes list create a playlist of five songs that you can create a ceremony around. Choose three songs, or pieces of music, that make you feel sad, one that fills you with energy, and a playful or silly tune. The three sad songs should be the ones that evoke a particularly sad event or period in your life, or remind you of a departed loved one. Ones that make you (or help you) cry or sob. Ones that get you every time. The song that fills you with energy can be anything that does just that. You can call this your power song. Finally complete the playlist with a silly or playful tune, such Monty Python's *Always look on the bright side of life*.

When you are ready to play all five songs one after the other, take an object from your altar that seems appropriate and go into darkness. Hold onto this object and visualise the person or situation it or the songs represent, as the first three sad tunes play. Allow yourself to go deep into any emotion that comes up and release it. When the power tune is heard move the object to the other hand and energise yourself. Feel positive life affirming energy filling both you and the object. You may want to move, sway or dance with this song and the energy imparted. What uplifting thoughts and positive emotions are now flowing around the situation or person your altar object or the sad songs represent? When the final silly track is played, bring yourself back to a place of balance and lightness, allowing all the negative and positive energies to dissipate. Try to finish with a smile on your face, and wherever the songs took you, give thanks. How does your altar object feel now? Does it still represent what you thought or has that changed? Over time emotions around the songs may change. Update the list as and when you wish.

Movement and shaking

Using music to help you move, to lose yourself within, is a great way to let go, and even go into a form of trance. A tribal backing track of drumming, rattling or similar, with few, if any, words allows you to connect with your body, shift energy and calm the mind chatter, rather than go into the emotions a song writer has desired to communicate when writing words and melodies.

With appropriate music playing move however you see fit, being mindful of your body. Try flowing movements, shaking, dance steps or simple jumping up and down. Try going barefoot and being on the land if possible. Tune into the music and visualise as you see fit. Maybe releasing, shaking off negativity in some way, connecting to others both in the present and the past, connecting to *Mother Earth* or the Universe. Give yourself permission to go wherever the music and your body take you.

Healing beats

Life would mean very little without beats, without a rhythm to dance to, a pulse to keep us on track or to denote the cycles of our lives, from day to night, the phases of the moon, to the changing of the seasons as our planet keeps its regular orbit around our star.

Beats and rhythms are everywhere. Starting within the womb, surrounded by fluid and in darkness, the mother's heartbeat is the soundtrack to the first nine months of our lives. This rhythmic sound is so comforting and familiar that it is used by new parents to help their little one(s) sleep, made evident by the number of womb sound videos available online.

Our heartbeat is also a valued ally throughout the rest of our life, letting us know when we are scared or startled, by wanting to jump out of our chest, pumping hard to prepare us for fight or flight, becoming a calming focus for our mind when drifting into meditation, fluttering when meeting someone we love, and seemingly stopping or breaking when we have to let them go. We hear it's beats in our ears when we overexert ourselves physically, telling us to slow down and then finally, when the beat stops, our time is up.

So look after your heart as best you can. It is your connection to the rhythm of life.

———————

Sight

Using light and immersing ourselves in various colours of the spectrum can have a profound effect on our emotional state and, as a consequence, our well being. The following are just a few of the many colour and light exercises that can be tried.

Colour immersion

Works of art that use blocks of colour (maybe even just one colour) on a large canvas, often win acclaim and elicit disdain, in equal measure. Why should a six foot square canvas painted orange be of any artistic value? Try standing near it, being engulfed by this colour. The colour can almost be felt when deeply looked into. One of the most profound colour experiences I have had was at an art installation in the UK, where a wall of electronic screens glowed with a block of colour, changing slowly over time from one colour to another. The screens were so large that when standing in front of them, all that could be seen was the colour they were emitting. A total immersion in this luminous energy. Afloat and adrift within it. It felt as though the colour had penetrated my whole body and I was one with it; every part of my anatomy vibrating in harmony with the colour.

Light boxes, coloured lens glasses and virtual goggles are available that can give a similar immersive experience. A cheap alternative is to view the world through a filter or piece of coloured plastic or acetate, or to gaze at blocks of colour in the form of coloured paper or card, or downloading coloured screen savers or similar for use on a laptop, tablet or phone. Gazing softly at a sunset, or laying on the ground and looking up at the blue sky, are also great ways to lose yourself in colour.

According to eastern tradition the major organs are directly linked to our internal energy centres, known as chakras, and the use of colour is one of the ways to help bring them into balance. Try visualising a cloud of each colour swirling around and through your body. However, as we are not just a heart and mind, but a digestive tract, nervous system, glands, bones, muscle, etc., all functioning together, allow the colours to move and merge as you work with them. The descriptions below are only a guide, so use your intuition, as we all react differently and to varying degrees to each of the colours.

> **Red** - an energising colour, known to loosen, open and release stiffness and constrictions. Useful for anaemia and blood related conditions.

Orange - has a freeing action upon the mind and body. Orange is a warm colour, the colour of the setting sun. It can help to bring about new ideas and can be helpful in dealing with surplus sexual expression.

Yellow - associated with strengthening the nerves and mind. A good colour for those who suffer from a nervous disposition.

Green - universal healing colour. Good for blood pressure and issues of the heart. It has an energising and soothing effect.

Blue - A soothing colour used for ailments and constrictions associated with speech and communication.

Indigo - It is known to purify the mind. Good for dealing with ailments within the eyes and ears, and stabilising mental problems.

Violet - colour of spirit, not generally used for physical conditions. Good for opening and expanding psychic pathways.

White - White light is comprised of all the colours so is often associated with perfection and God/Goddess. Can be used for direct connection to the divine, general self healing and replacing released negative energies.

Silver/Gold - Shimmering and reflective these colours are wonderful for energising the body and mind, or reflecting away negative energies. Useful in attracting wealth and abundance.

Converse with the body

The cells in our body are constantly being created, albeit at different rates depending on the type of cell. For example stomach and intestinal cells are replaced every five or so days, skin cells every two to four weeks, and liver cells every five months. Cells in the skeletal system regenerate almost constantly, but the complete process takes a full ten years, although the renewal process slows down as we age[11].

If cells are being created all the time then the more we can be in a pleasant and comfortable state the higher the chance the cells will be created in a healthy way. Conversely, if we are in a constant state of stress or agitation then the cells created are open to taking on this negative energy, or to mutate when regenerating. Does it seem possible that, for example, during a period of prolonged stress certain vulnerable cells could mutate into cancerous ones? There is no proof of this, according to the UK National Health Service from trials that have been conducted, but like many esoteric ideas, I suggest using your own discernment.

When in meditation talk to you body, focussing on each area as you do so. Create a dialogue between you and your individual parts. Pose questions and wait for answers. For example ask, "How are you heart?", "Can I do anything for you lungs?", or "Liver, what should I do to help you today?" Try asking the varying parts of your body what colour you need to work with to help clear blockages and keep each area healthy, being mindful that this may change each time you do the exercise.

Visualise the colour floating in a ball in front of your face. Gently inhale this colourful energy and allow it to move to where it is

---

[11] Chris Opfer, *Does your body really replace itself every seven years?*, Updated Apr 2021, *Howsstuffworks.com.*

needed, bathing and soothing the organ or area. With the exhale see the same colour blown out, but now carrying away any blockage or energetic impurities. Repeat this cycle of inhale and exhale keeping the energetic colour flowing.

Running the rainbow

This is a lovely exercise connecting not only to the beauty and colour of a rainbow but also linking to the four classical elements, as a rainbow is the product of the Sun's energy in the form of light (*fire*), refracted in the atmosphere (*air*), through raindrops (*water*) that have formed around dust particles *(earth)*. It is one of the most beautiful sights in nature and can be used spiritually as the gift it is.

The rainbow is an arc of light, as seen from our perspective (it is actually a circle if viewed from above), with a beginning and end. But, as we know, we can never reach either, and never find the pot of gold at the end of the rainbow. This is true, but when working energetically with rainbows we can change the rules.

Find stillness either sitting or laying down and visualise a rainbow, with you sat at one end of it. Bring each colour down in turn, filling yourself with each. Surround yourself with an aura of each colour. A *Ready Brek*[12] glow of red, orange, yellow, green, sky blue, indigo and violet.

How does each colour feel? Are any out of balance? If one feels weaker than the other expand it; make it stronger, more vibrant, more energetic. Maybe a reason for the imbalance will be shown to you. Now allow the full spectrum of colours to flow down into your body, filling you with a myriad of colour; rainbows swirling within

---

[12] *Ready Brek* is a breakfast cereal that has had UK advertising campaigns, starting in the 1970s, showing the children who ate it surrounded by a warm orange glow.

you. Allow the colours to move and blend, swim and pulse throughout your physical and energetic body, finding their own balance.

Finally come to a sitting position with hands on your thighs or knees, palms facing up, and visualise a rainbow coming out of one palm, arcing over and going into the other. Vary the width of your hands and allow the rainbow to change size appropriately. Allow the colours to move from your hands and into the rest of your body. Again feel the energy, beauty and healing power. Fill every space with a spectrum of colour.

Play with these techniques, and see how they feel to you. Vary the size of the rainbow, the colour intensity, add weather too if that feels right, as there is always rain and sun for a rainbow to appear, often after a storm. Feel your chaotic, storm energies subside and dissipate as the rainbow appears, as the colours soothe you. A rainbow can then take on a more profound meaning next time you see one.

Using spells and potions
Note: Safety warning

Spells, although often having a negative connotation associated with them, are to my mind, reinforced prayers, asking for help in a ceremonial way, by combining them with a common object such as a candle or wooden stick (wand). The spell, or the purpose of the spell, can be scratched into a candle before lighting, or carved into a stick before being burnt. Alternatively a spell can be written on a piece of paper which can then be burnt ceremonially. The mixing of herbs, plants or other natural items, to form potions for healing and for use in spells is a whole subject on its own and not covered in any detail in this book. Medicines come from the natural world so I suggest concocting potions for spells and healing is founded on strong roots (literally).

Your own potion can be created without any knowledge of herbalism by using medically non active ingredients and mixing them in a ceremonial way. Use a decorative pot or jar and bless any water or liquid used. Imbibe the mixture with positive energy and loving thoughts by adding pleasant smelling liquids, flower petals, leaves, sweets or cake decorations, and anything you feel would add to the potency of the mixture based on your intention. This, in the Q'ero tradition I have been taught, is known as a *limpia* (*clean* in Spanish), a potion filled with love, and, as the name suggests, to be used to help clean the soul. The *limpia* can then be used for blessings, anointing or pouring on your body, sacred objects or the earth, but please do not drink it. The Q'ero use another method to create potions that can be taken internally but that is not covered in this book.

Always make any potion or spell positive. Like one would a prayer. Never make it negative, with the intent of doing harm to another. As with any spiritual work, if you are asking for something negative to happen to someone, be prepared for it to come back to you, and not in a good way. This is not the purpose of using spiritual energy, prayer, spells, potions or similar. It is about weaving a wonderful life for you, your family, your community, the more-than-human world and ultimately all life on this planet.

Creation

Creation is the most powerful force in the Universe. From the Big Bang to conception. It drives expansion. It is the essence of the Universe. Being creative, in whatever way you choose, is beneficial to your mental, physical and spiritual well-being. Anything artistic, whatever you can lose yourself in, or makes your world a little more beautiful, is a wonderful use of time.

There are a myriad ways to be creative, not only as an artistic expression but in all you do. Perhaps look at areas in your life where you may feel a little stale or stuck. Try new methods or techniques, incorporate new ideas, reviewing how others do something similar (online videos are great for this) and see if anything resonates with you.

Create your symbol

Symbols can bypass the consciousness and enter the sub-consciousness. Hence the power of corporate logos and marketing.

Write a sentence describing what you want your symbol to stand for. Maybe it is a desire or dream, or just to represent yourself. Maybe use the letters of your name. When you have your words remove the vowels and repeated letters and reduce it to the key letters or initials. Rearrange the remaining letters into a symbol that resonates with your intention. If nothing is forthcoming just play with lines and keep moving the shapes around until you find a symbol you are happy with. Write this symbol out a number of times and become familiar with it. Then be creative with it. Carve it into wood, paint it, draw it, create jewellery with it or put it on a t-shirt. Use it in ceremony. Imbibe it with power. It is your symbol, play with it.

Share the love exercise

Sit in front of a mirror and look into your eyes. Let love radiate from your eyes into the the eyes of your reflection. Feel the love emanate from your heart. Let any negative thoughts go and keep focusing on generating love. How easy is this for you to do? Are there any blocks? Do you feel silly or are you hung up on how you look? Can you see past the physical? Work on this until you can. Feel the love, a warm, fuzzy, peaceful love, and expand it from your heart out through your eyes. When you feel connected to the love in your heart, the love you are radiating, take a moment to accept the love for yourself. You are worthy to both give and receive love.

Let the love, and the feeling of love, encompass your whole body, then overflow and radiate out, to cover the space you are in, the building, the street, the town and beyond. Feel it radiate to those around you, your friends and family, the community, the country, and out onto the whole planet. Bathe everything in love. Imagine it as a wave of loving heart threads radiating out from you, carrying this love out far and wide. Visualise and feel it being received by all those you are sending it to, by the people, the plants and animals, by *Mother Earth* and *Father Sky*. Sense the gratitude come back, in return for this gift of love you have freely given.

While still in this bubble of radiating love bring your focus back to yourself and send love to areas of your body you think may need it, to parts of your psyche you wish to love on, to any worries or troublesome situations, to people and animals suffering, or any worldwide concerns. Send love to wherever you feel it is needed, from your unlimited supply. Take a moment to connect with the ancestors and share the love with them and feel their love in return. Connect to your parents, grandparents, then great grandparents and beyond. Connect to the countless generations. Finally, if you are drawn to, send love to any spirit guides or teachers, gurus or deities, as a thank you for their help and guidance.

This exercise can be done with another person, or in pairs within a group situation. Begin by sitting facing each other at arms length and look into each other's eyes, repeating the word "love" in your mind, and showing this love in your eyes. Don't look for love in the other person's eyes, only radiate love from yours. Keep doing this, and continue to look even if you feel uncomfortable. Keep going beyond any inhibitions. This sharing of love is open and honest with no strings attached. No promises being made. Just a pure exchange of love energy. Love is an abundant energy, so you can keep giving it without ever losing it. In fact the more you give the more your receive. So sharing your love is not being wasteful, and there is no need to receive any in return, as you can always generate more love energy. It is likely the other person will respond in kind and share their love, so the love energy will grow between you.

All manner of emotions may come up for one or both of you. Smiles, laughter, playfulness, desires, or maybe sadness, painful memories or heartbreak. Play with it but try to spend at least least ten minutes in this space, finishing in a positive place. When completed embrace if you wish, and be in gratitude for what each has shared. No words other than thank you are needed. Don't feel pressured into saying any more once the exercise is over, unless you wish to. This is not a romantic or sexual exercise so it does not mater if the other person is your partner or not. It is very empowering, albeit a little unsettling, to do with a stranger in a group setting but well worth getting over any inhibitions to give it a go.

Ancestral honouring

"You're just like your father", or "I sound just like my mother", are commonly spoken phrases throughout households in the UK. We inherit so much, not just physical characteristics, but our mannerisms, behaviours and beliefs. No upbringing is perfect and it is up the individual, normally once in adulthood, to recognise and make changes if they need to. This is easier said than done as inherited patterns become ingrained, behaviours change into habits, and genes (currently) are ours for life. List the traits of your parents, both good and bad. Which are in you?

Create your own ceremony of thanks for the gifts they have given you. Be thankful not only for life but all the love and teachings, care and support, safety and security provided. Also thank them for the not so good things that you are now ready to forgive and release, be it their anger, pain, quick temper, apologetic attitude, lack of self esteem, constant judging, overbearing nature, etc. Let go of anything negative, perhaps with one or more of the exercises from *The South*. Having an object, or objects, on your altar that represents one or both of your parents is normally beneficial as there is often much to work upon in this area. If you feel that you had a relatively good upbringing it is still worth having a mother and father object as it strengthens your connection to them and honours the love they have (or had) for you, and the love you have for them.

Female lineage connection

Use your mother object from your altar, or an object that represents female energy to you, whether you are female or male. If you are male, then do this exercise with a focus on female energy, the female lineage of you family.

Visualise your mother standing behind you, her hands on your shoulders. It doesn't matter if she is alive or in spirit. Imagine she is with you today for this ceremony. Continue with your female lineage standing behind her, ancestral mothers with hands on their daughter's shoulders going back as far as you can imagine. It does not matter if you never knew your mother, grandmother, great grandmother, etc. Just visualise women standing in a line, one behind the other. Link into this lineage. What is being passed down? What do the mothers wish for their daughters? What teaching and wisdom is being passed down? How does this feel? Then, if you have a daughter (or daughters), imagine her (or them) standing in front of you, your hands on her (or their) shoulders. What are you passing on? What have you not passed on? Why not? Where are the blocks?

Do the same for any granddaughters or great granddaughters. If you do not have a daughter, imagine you do and visualise putting your hands on her shoulders. How does that feel? Do you want to raise a daughter? What would your hopes and dreams be for her?

When you are ready visualise yourself turning and facing your mother, putting your hands on her shoulders, with hers on yours. Can you look her in the eyes? What is this like? What comes up? Do either of you want to say anything to each other? Finally thank her. Thank her for the gift of life, for carrying you in her womb, and all she has given and provided for you. Continue with this gratitude and extend it to all of your lineage going backwards and forwards. Thanking the women that came before and the women to come after you. Look to include the mothers from you fathers side of the family too if you haven't already.

Male lineage connection

This can be done separately or straight after the female lineage exercise. For this use your father object from your altar, or an object that represents male energy to you, whether you are male or female. If you are female carry out this exercise with a focus on male energy, the male lineage in your ancestry.

In a similar way to the female lineage exercise, visualise your father standing behind you, his hands on your shoulders. It doesn't matter if he is alive or in spirit. Imagine he is with you today for this ceremony. Then visualise his father stood behind him with his hands on your father's shoulders. Continue with your male lineage, your ancestral fathers with their hands on their son's shoulders going back as far as you can imagine. Don't worry about accurately seeing their faces, just allow the images to come. If there are no images just sense this long male line. Link into this lineage. What is being passed down? What does each father wish for his son? What teachings or wisdom is being shared? How does this feel?

Then, if you have a son (or sons), imagine him (or them) standing in front of you, your hands on his (or their) shoulders. What are you passing on? What energy is there between you? What have you not passed on? What have you not shared? Where are the blocks? Do the same for all grandsons or great grandsons. If you do not have a son, imagine you do and put your hands on his shoulders. How does that feel? Do you want to raise a son? What would your hopes and dreams be for him?

When you are ready visualise yourself turning and facing your father, putting your hands on each others shoulders. Can you look him in the eyes? What is this like? What comes up? Do either of you want to say anything to each other? Finally thank him. Thank him for the gift of life and all he has given and provided you. Continue with this gratitude and extend it to all of your lineage going backwards and forwards. Thanking the men that came before and the men to come after you. Then go on to include the fathers on your mother's side of the family.

Note: Ceremonies have known to have taken place 35,000 years ago and it is thought our brain size has been the same as it is now for much longer. In fact the brain has been the same size for 300,000 years and the same shape for 30,000 - 100,000 years.[13] If we take the figure of 35,000 years as a (conservative) baseline for homosapiens similar to us, then the number of previous generations is approximately two thousand, based on an average age of eighteen for a woman to give birth. So to visualise your ancestors would require a line behind you of almost two thousand people, each with their hands on the others shoulders, stretching back for well over a kilometre, or close to one mile.

Two thousand generations as capable and undoubtedly as curious and intelligent, in their own way, as modern man. What has been learnt by these generations that has been lost? What has been learnt by those that were far more connected and in tune with the land and the energies the earth, rocks, oceans, and all life produce? Over these millennia what evolution has taken place? What changes have human beings undergone over two thousand generations?

Also intricate mandalas have been created from different coloured sand by some Buddhist monks as part of their spiritual practice, often to honour those that have gone before, as they believe we are made from grains of our ancestors.

---

[13] Neubauer, Hublin and Gunz, *The evolution of modern human brain shape*, published in *Science Advances*, 24 Jan 2018.

Additional exercises:

1) Connect with both parents and all of your ancestors
You may wish to expand the above visualisations, before you close the space, to embrace both parents, visualising them with one hand on each of your shoulders. Then in turn, their parents before them and so on, fanning back through your complete ancestry. Feel your lineage flow into you. Let the energy build inside you. What are the teachings? Is there balance between male and female?

You are the result of millions of years of evolution, and currently stand at the forefront of this evolution. It has taken 13.7 billion years, the age of the known Universe, to reach this point. All that history, all that evolutionary adaptation, has culminated in you. You have every right to be here and you are very special indeed.

Note: If there is an adoption in your family history then include this additional branch of your tree. Both the biological and non-biological parents played a role. Bare in mind too that if we are going back say two thousand generations then it is quite likely we all have an adoption in our lineage somewhere. We also are likely be linked to the whole gamut of humanity from nobility to pauper, priest to thief, builder to philosopher, healer to life taker.

2) Cutting the ancestral ties
Whilst carrying out the ancestral connection work outlined above you may wish to transmute any negative energies or inherited traits that no longer serve. A simple way to cut these ancestral ties is by energetically cutting the negative threads that are woven through your lineage, through you and even passed onto your offspring.

Imagine a chord of negative energy coming into you from your ancestors, passing through you and out in front of you. Cut this chord off, both entering and leaving you, using a visualised sword, knife, energy beam, or similar. See it disintegrate, shatter off into sparkles of light, dispersing into the ether. Pull out any strands from your body and blow them away as dust in the air. Feel the negative connection being severed and dissolving into the ether.

———————

Inner child work

Take time to remember and get to know your inner child. *Little you*. You from a baby, through infancy to childhood. What are your earliest memories? Try to fill in the the rest of the time from when you were conceived to your first memories. Where were you born? What was the house and area like? Do you have photos? Have you spoken to your parents about your birth and infancy? If not why not? If they are not around to speak to is there another family member you can ask? Revisit places of your childhood. Old haunts, schools, parks, friends/aunts/uncles/grandparents houses that you frequented, places where incidents you remember happened. Where do your childhood memories want to lead you back to? Write about these places if it is not practical to visit. What emotions come up? Release any negativity. Rekindle the joys and positives of your childhood.

Write a letter to your inner child. Start it with "Dear Little [insert your name]". What do you want to say to your younger self, around the age of four or five, *Little you*? What hopes and dreams did you have for your life looking back? What advice and teachings do you want to share? What warnings, if any? What apologies do you want to make? Is there any regret over failed plans or broken promises? Any sorrow or guilt? Be as honest and open as you can, allowing the emotion to flow. If tears come let them, let them fall onto the paper you write on, adding another level of emotional intensity to this deeply personal process. When finished put the letter in an envelope and address it, "To Little [insert your name]".

Then write a letter from your inner child to you. This time, however, the letter needs to be written using your non-normal hand. This will take time, allowing you to focus on the words and the emotions that arise, and probably make the writing look like that of a child. Start the letter with "Dear Big [insert your name]." What does *Little you* want to say to *Big you*? What were your dreams, aspirations, hopes for the future? How did *Little you* feel? Did they feel safe when young, or vulnerable? What emotions were going on? Was there fear? Was there love? What was *Little you's* relationship to your parents like? Take yourself back to your younger self, even if only in spirit if the memories are too distant. Embody this inner child energy and write from the heart. When finished put this letter into an envelope marked, "To Big [insert your name]".

You now have two letters, one from you to your inner child, and another from your inner child to you. Keep these letters for as long as you wish, to review and contemplate upon. Are there any commonalities, any themes running through both? What areas can you work upon? When you feel ready, let go of the letters, either by burning them in a ceremonial way, or by posting them to the Universe, ensuring they cannot find their way back to you.

Childhood photo board and video story

Collate together photographs of yourself, from a baby through to adulthood, creating a collage on a large piece of card, cork board or similar. Let them tell the story of you growing physically. Use the most powerful pictures, good or bad. What emotion does this bring up? Are there any photos that exhibit a different emotion to one that you thought you had at that time? Maybe during a difficult period you feel that you were constantly unhappy, but the photos you have from that time clearly show you were happy. What does this tell you? How do the emotions you pick up from the photos fit with how you looked physically? Are you comfortable with how you looked? Did you feel comfortable at the time?

If your life has been documented via video camera or smartphone then try editing together a video montage of your birth to adolescence and adulthood, again collating the good and bad, and noticing what emotions are triggered.

Childlike vs childish and asking for help

Being childish means behaving like a child and reacting as a child would, with such behaviour in an adult linked to a lack of emotional intelligence if displayed regularly. Even so, this behaviour can often be witnessed in successful and prominent people across the globe, from world leaders and heads of corporations, to sports people and celebrities. A tantrum is still a tantrum at whatever age it is stamped out. Being childlike is different. It is being in that space of innocence, wonder and awe, a place of trust and exploration, where discovery and adventure comes naturally, as it does to children.

Firstly, to overcome the societal and cultural pressures of having to behave like an adult, give yourself permission to be a child once again. Allow yourself the time and space to explore what it means to be a child again. Connect to your inner child. If you have written the letters to and from your inner child, then the connection should be clearer and easier to make.

A childlike state naturally opens us up to the signs of the Universe, the messages and energies that come to us daily. In this sate we absorb information and experiences, just as children do. So try babbling like a toddler, crawl around like an infant (noticing the new perspective), sit and play with a stick, or just stare at a flower. Watch the ants, marvel at a spiders web, lose yourself in a painting or dive into a photo. Dress up as a cowboy, a princess, an astronaut. Play football and pretend to score the winning goal in the world cup. Visualise yourself on stage winning the final of a talent show. Splash in a puddle or skip through the woods kicking up autumnal leaves. Play with life a little. We were all children once and still are children at heart, so remember how to play.

Children have no problem asking for help, as they instinctively want to learn. Asking for help reinforces the fact that we do not know everything, it shows humility. As we are all children spiritually, why not ask for help from your subconscious, your spiritual guides, or the divine. Wouldn't it or they want to help? However, as we are conscious and have free will, it is up to us to ask for help, and, just as importantly, to wait for, and be open to, the reply.

Simple methods of asking for help are prayer, meditation, shamanic journeying, letter writing, conversing with nature or even pilgrimage to a significant place. A pilgrimage doesn't necessarily have to be to a religious site, it can just as easily be to a place in nature you are drawn to. Following in the footsteps of others who have held the quest for help in their heart, can bolster your own determination to find answers for yourself.

Praying, asking God for help, is fine if you believe in God. If you have doubt, or do not believe, then you need to find a way to move into a similar place of call and response, of asking for help and listening for the answer. A similar place of learning.

We learn best from teachers, because as children we instinctively believed what was being told to us by authority figures. They were trusted and we realised that grown ups were trying to help us. Sadly, however, that trust can be broken. If you have ever experienced such a betrayal then, if you haven't already, I strongly suggest working on this, to clear as much of the emotional charge, negative thought patterns and unconscious energy around it. The exercises around letting go, forgiveness and inner child work will offer some assistance with this.

Therefore, when asking for help with an issue, put yourself into a child like state and play with the process or exercise, but remember to listen for the answer, and do not be surprised if it seems comical, fantastical, or presented in a way that your inner child would understand, and as such, may seem rather simplistic to you as an adult.

Being childlike, as opposed to childish, can have it's rewards. Never lose contact to that inner child, and a youthful outlook on life. It keeps the journey fresh and joyful, and acts as a beacon to those that cross your path.

Those that have gone before

We have recorded our thoughts and ideas, our philosophies and opinions, our stories and advice, with the written word; firstly on clay and stone, then papyrus scrolls and, since the invention of the printing press, in newspapers and books. Most recently our words can be stored and shared digitally, or even recorded as audio and video media, adding emotion and colour to what we want to say. What cannot be recorded though are feelings. Only the words, music or visual representations that try to describe these feelings. By taking action, experiencing and discovering things for ourselves, we can explore and, to some degree, replicate these feelings, understanding a little more as to why certain spiritual practices or exercises may have been passed down through the generations. Through replication and practice we find our connection to the past strengthened.

There are those that have gone before, who have sat where you have sat, looked out from where you have looked out, thought about what you have thought about. As new as every day may seem to us, as unique we believe we are as individuals, there have been many others who have felt similarly to us. So try gazing in wonder at a sunset or the full moon, and connect to the millions who have done so before you, or swim under a waterfall and feel the magic of those that have previously swam in that place, or may even have been blessed there.

It is, in some part, from the activities of those that have gone before, their energetic echo, that places become sacred, buildings holy. This energy builds in these sites, especially in beautiful places in nature. This is akin to what Rupert Sheldrake coined as *morphic resonance* - an inherited memory passed down through the generations that builds up the spiritual energy of a place. Take a moment when in such places to feel the connection to the past, to those that have gone before, allowing gratitude to flow.

Ancestors around the fire

People have sat around fire for as long as there have been people. Fire has provided light, warmth, security, and a means of cooking food. It is a place of gathering and sharing. A place of ceremony and celebration. A place of story telling and imagination. Fire has been gazed upon in wonderment, and enraptured many a captivated mind for generations. One could even label it nature's TV, to give fire a modern spin.

Either light a candle or, if you have access to one, light a real fire and sit in front of that. Get comfortable and allow your gaze to dwell on the candle flame or fire before gently softening your focus or closing you eyes. Sense, feel or imagine yourself in nature, sat in a clearing next to an open fire. In your visualisation gaze softly into the fire, feeling it's warmth. Sense the connection to all fires around the world, and to all fires that have ever been, sensing the multitude of people who have sat around them.

Begin by giving thanks to those that have come before you, those that have walked the earth where you are now, and maybe at some point in time, sat around an open fire where, or very near to where, you are physically doing this visualisation. The UK, for example, has been inhabited for at least thirteen thousand years and I suggest many fires have been lit within eye shot of almost every square metre of land.

Start by inviting your own family, alive or in spirit, along with their ancestors to come and share the fire with you. Imagine them sitting in rings around you and the fire, the first ring comprised of your immediate family, the second their parents and so on outwards. Keep imagining rings of ancestors, present with you in this liminal place, coming to share the fire with you. There may be non humans wanting to be there with you too; animals, deities, ascended masters, etc. Anyone or anything can turn up. Go back as far as you like and be swamped in the largest fire circle ever known, with you sat next to the fire in the centre.

All who have come, have come because of you. They have come for you. How does that make you feel? How do you think the ancestors feel about being there with you? Being honoured in such a way, being invited to a ceremonial fire. Put yourself in their shoes and look down upon yourself and this circle. Is there any wisdom they want to impart? Are there any messages?

Sit with this imagery, being aware of your feelings, and be in a place of gratitude. Know also that you have every right to be sat where you are and represent all who have gone before. Feel the love, feel the energy, and allow yourself to be humbled by it, by the privilege you have been given. You may wish to dance, sing, chant, drum or rattle in this fire circle, in your mind or maybe even wherever you are physically. Do so. Do whatever you feel is helpful in honouring your ancestors around this fire. Play with this. If something feels disrespectful or incorrect, stop doing it, apologise to those present and try something else. Mistakes, as has been said before, are OK and all part of learning and growing.

When you feel you have finished give a final thanks to those that have come to your fire, bring yourself out of your visualisation and open your eyes to gaze on your candle or real fire. Spend some time in gratitude in this space. To take this further try conducting your own fire ceremony (see *Mother Earth* section.)

Grandmother and grandfather energy

This energy emanates from a long lived person. A wise elder. Someone who has lived a full life, learnt from their mistakes, successfully raised children, helped the family and community, is full of wisdom (but still open to learning), has nothing to prove, has no need to compete, realises that everyone has a right to their own spirituality, is connected to their environment, laughs a lot, is generous, has a kind *lived in* face, is happy, content, and at peace with themselves.

Sound wonderful don't they. Can you tap into this energy? Do or did your own grandparents exhibit such energy? If they did then incorporate them in your meditation, otherwise invite imagined wonderful and benevolent grandmothers or grandfathers to come and be with you. Use the above fire visualisation or the stone circle journey from the *Shamanic Engineering* section to aid the connection. Feel worthy to absorb this wisdom. Allow it to embrace and engulf you. Give thanks for such a powerful birthright.

Ancestor box

If you have objects, trinkets or keepsakes from loved ones, try collecting them all together in a suitable box or container. This can then become your ancestor box. Having all of these items in one place can help dissolve past individual family ties, morphing them into general ancestral honouring, and help in the realisation that what has come down through your lineage, the gift of your life today, is only because of every single one of your ancestors. The whole of your lineage since the dawn of time. If there was a break in the chain you would not be here. You may want to keep this box on or near your altar. What stories do the items tell? Can any items be passed on or given away? If not why not? What advice would the ancestors the objects represent want to give you?

The East - **The bigger picture, vision, and dreams**

*"One doesn't discover new lands without consenting to
lose sight of the shore for a very long time."*
Andre Gide.

The East is represented by Eagle or Condor and is about looking at things from a different perspective, and seeing the bigger picture. Condor's sharp eyesight invites us to focus on our dreams, even if they seem far away, and shows us that we can see further when we fly high and gain a broad overview, reaching such heights seemingly effortlessly. Just as Condor soars high in the sky, in a world that we can only gaze at from the ground, *The East* is the direction where we begin to explore our connection to all that is above, to what is outside of us, more specifically to Great Mystery and the divine.

Do you know what you want? What are your dreams, your desires, your life goals? What steps have you made towards them? What needs to change? A Condor's viewpoint is forever moving as she soars across the skies. The ground below, however, is more static in nature. But even here over time erosion, fire, animal activity, human development, etc., all change the landscape. Nothing is static. Change is everywhere. We too can, and do, change.

What is your medicine?

In this case when referring to medicine I am not talking about a prescribed pill or tonic, but the characteristics and traits you possess that provide help and healing to yourself, your community and the world around you. What are you good at? What are your gifts? What is your arena? What were your parents gifts? Have you inherited any? Were you born to play an instrument, to sing, create art, grow things, organise, be a healer, make people laugh, be an accountant, a footballer, an engineer, a carer, a mother or father? Where does your passion lie? What you love, what you are drawn to, what you are good at, can be termed *your medicine*.

Singers have to sing, musicians have to play, dancers have to dance, comedians have to entertain people, sportsmen and women have to compete. It is clear, most obviously within the arts and sport, that some people were born to do what they do. Jimi Hendrix to play the guitar, Karen Carpenter to sing, Keith Moon to play the drums, George Best to play football, Robert De Niro to act, Mo Farah to run, Pablo Picasso to paint, or Shakespeare to write. These people, along with many others who had or have a passion for what they do, feel something more. A compulsion to do it, a necessity. They have to follow this calling or else they are depriving themselves of some part (perhaps a large part) of life as they see it. Playing the instrument, competing in their sport, immersing themselves in the character, or creating the art work is *in their blood*, a major component of who they are, and often when they feel most comfortable and confident expressing themselves.

We all have this to some extent, perhaps not as obvious or prevalent as those mentioned above, or others we can think of, but it is still there nonetheless. Our own medicine. So what is yours? Immersed in what action does your heart beat fastest? What would you do if you could do anything? What do you have to do?

Maybe some of the most potent examples of people embodying their medicine had something special. Lets call it a genius gene. Something different from us mere mortals that helped drive them to express their talent, their medicine, as far as they possibly could; to break new ground, create something different or achieve new heights, raising the bar in their field. It is a driver of evolution. Pushing the limits, so that the next generation can push them still further. Note however, having this gene, or more accurately this desire, should not be a goal in and of itself. Many who have pushed themselves can be consumed by this aspirational behaviour, becoming perhaps obsessive, delusional or deeply depressed at never achieving the unattainable goals they set themselves. 'Live fast, die young' is not a motto of the enlightened soul. So living your dreams, following your heart, as good advice as it is, must be tempered with a healthy outlook and consideration for your body and mind. For sure, follow your passion but not at the expense of your health.

Once you have identified your medicine look to embrace it within your life as best you can. How can it be manifested within your vocation, your home, your family, or where you choose to live? Find ways to share it as much as possible so that it's benefit can be felt by many. Work with your medicine, not against it. Often though to work with your medicine, to give it the focus it deserves, means removing some of the clutter from your mind and life. Making space for the new. Hopefully some of the exercises from *The South, The West* and *The North* have helped with this clearing and healing process, opening the way to go deeper by flying higher, as Condor teaches.

What is normal?

It is deemed culturally acceptable to want to fit in, to belong. We are regularly told that we are social animals and it is beneficial to our health to be around others, to interact and have relationships, as was highlighted during the coronavirus pandemic, when social interactions were curtailed and feelings of isolation widespread. We like to be in our comfort zone, by being around those that are similar to us, that maybe look, sound and dress like us, perhaps even hold similar views. Many people want to belong, to be part of something bigger than themselves, and be part of a tribe of sorts. This may shed some light on the pleasure (and pain) of supporting a particular sporting team, trends in fashion, or even getting a similar tattoo to others. Conversely, and more seriously, when people are deemed not to fit in, individuals or whole groups of people, can be open to trolling, verbal abuse, persecution, physical violence or even the threat of death, from their tormentors. This bigotry and persecution is likely to result in, at the very least, mental trauma, but also physical health issues, suicidal thoughts or fleeing for ones life to another place or country and seeking asylum.

We are, of course, all human and in that sense similar, but we also know that we are unique, and are probably glad we are, even if at times we may feel that we don't fit in. However, being different is an essential part of being normal; that is, normal from a statistical point of view.

The figure below illustrates how a group of people (or population) is measured against any characteristic or category. The characteristic is along the bottom, or X axis, and the quantity, or number of occurrences, on the vertical, or Y axis. In general, most populations produce a bell shaped curve when measured against most characteristics. This indicates that the majority of the population are towards the middle, are nearer the average, whilst at the extremes of the characteristic there are fewer occurrences. For example, if the category on the bottom axis was male height then the majority of men would be between 5'3" and 6'4" (1.6m-1.93m). There would be fewer people at the smaller and taller sizes, reducing down to just one person at either end of the spread. In 2014, according to Wikipedia, the world's shortest man was Chandra Bahadur Dangi, from Nepal, at 0.55m (21.5 inches), and the world's tallest man Sultan Kosen, from Turkey, was 2.67m (8 foot 9 inches). All other men would be in between when comparing their height.

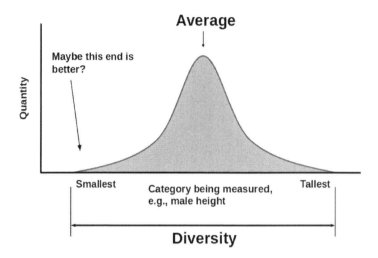

The people towards the extremes of this curve, the shortest and tallest, have undoubtedly had various comments throughout their lives about their size. Sadly these comments may be negative and spiteful, reinforcing to the receiver that they are not normal. However, this is not statistically true because the whole of the population under the line is *normal*. This is what a normal population looks like. It has two thinner tails and a large middle hump. The hump is where the average lies, where the mean, median and mode averages sit. Being on the edge, in the tails, is still normal, just further away from the average. Further away from the middle, can be thought of as sometimes positive and sometimes negative, just as perhaps being average can have a dual meaning.

Being further to one direction or another again can have its merits and drawbacks. In the height example maybe it is better to be towards the left tail in some instances, as if one is smaller than average then there are advantages to be had with regards leg room on planes, a likely lower spend on food and never having to worry about bumping into low doorways or ceilings.

There are advantages and disadvantages to both extremes and yes, they are different from the average, but still very much normal. The spread shows how diverse a population is, with the whole of the group in question fitting under the curve and, most importantly, statistically normal.

So even if you feel you are one of a kind you are still normal because you fit the statistical spread. Someone has to be at the limit. Why not you? Yes maybe you are not average in certain areas, such as character traits or physical measurements, but that is life. That is variation. And it is normal.

Who are you? The roles we play in life

If you were asked the question, "Who are you?", how would you respond? Your name probably? Your sex? Your nationality? How about your job or marital status? Are these the things define you? Look around your home. What represents you? What does your home, the objects you own, the area where you live, the country you are living in or even the culture your are from, reflect back to you? What do these things say about who you think you are?

Write out a list of answers to the question "Who are you?" Here are few to get you going. A woman, a plumber, a housekeeper, a friend, a carer, an animal, a collection of atoms, a student, a teacher. Be creative and see how many you can come up with.

This list is likely to be much longer than you originally thought. It shows that we have, and play out, many roles in life. In fact we are much more than we think we are and therefore are likely to have more gifts and skills than perhaps we thought we did.

As human beings we are incredible creatures, amazing machines that convert food to fuel, continually grow and replace cells, heal ourselves from injuries and illnesses, adapt to many environments and conditions, are water proof but can breathe, are heat resistant but can sweat to sustain an optimal operating temperature, and have an internal pump that operates 24/7, for upwards of a hundred years in some cases. Then we have our brain; that collection of billions of neurons that spark with electricity allowing us to learn, to dream, to analyse, to discern, to remember, to calculate, to be aware, and, arguably, where our consciousness resides.

But for all our amazing physiology, biology and chemistry we can easily be enslaved and indoctrinated; be moulded or influenced by our upbringing, our surroundings and our own thoughts. As Henry Ford said, "Whether you think you can, or you think you can't - you're right."

Are your core beliefs yours? How many are inherited or imposed upon you by circumstance? Looking through the roles you have played or are playing, which ones are who you want to be? Can you let go of the ones holding you back, the ones that no longer serve you? Try letting go of the roles that you no longer want in a ceremonial way, by writing them on individual pieces of paper or sticks, and burning them in a fire. Alternatively use a candle to light them and drop the burning paper into a flame proof dish.

What roles do you want to keep, the roles you love, the ones that are truly you. What new roles would you like to explore, learn or embody? Create another list of new roles, aspirational ones, linked maybe to your vision board (see later) and write an affirmation (also see later) around them. Try being creative with these roles. Create an artwork to reflect them, or write a song or piece of music that encapsulates them. Begin to dream your world into being.

You may feel anger doing any of the above, when you realise that so much of who you are isn't really you, or at least the real you that you now want to embody. This is OK and understandable as you have to realise that the normal way of raising children, through adolescence and into adult life, for the majority of the population, is common and goes largely unchallenged. As creatures of habit we bring up children as we were brought up, maybe changing a few things that we we remember not liking as children, but by and large fitting in to the societal norms. Forgive your parents, they knew no better. Forgive the community and culture you were raised in, as this has been moulded over many years by people who also knew no better.

No government has the vision or ability to create a utopian world, a world perhaps portrayed in fantasy or science fiction, a world where humanity has moved beyond power struggles, money, ownership, inequalities, colour or creed. This utopia is currently only found in small pockets around the world, in enlightened families and communities. However the ideals they live by can be embraced by anyone and, in my opinion, are actually within every human heart on the planet, albeit buried or hidden.

It is only each of us as individuals that can create the joy of life. Created through our thoughts, expressed in our behaviours and finally realised by our actions. No authority, no committee, company or government will do this for us. It is a bottom up approach that is required, not top down. So, as Jesus is reported to have said on the cross, "Forgive them, for they do not know", certainly still holds true today.

The falsehoods and misinformation have increased in the modern internet age, so each day it is becoming more of a necessity to really discern what you are being fed as news, information and knowledge. The web offers an onslaught of opinion, conjecture, blatant and veiled lies, but also meaningless trivia, useless information, and a myriad of bizarre, fatuous, and time wasting content on social media and video streaming platforms, containing little of value to the enquiring mind. The so called influencers and celebrities, that self publicise or promote themselves, and their sponsored products, are certainly having an effect on the (mainly young) people that spend hours a day watching, and in some cases idolising and emulating, these web celebrities. Again any intellectual nourishment is debatable.

The mental health problem that is on the increase partly due to this bombardment of conflicting information and behaviours, such as the ridiculous ideas on beauty and health, that can lead to a lack of identity, increased stress, and imposed (self or otherwise) unachievable standards, will not be solved by any form of government intervention, filtering or censoring. It has to come from educating children, and adults, about self worth, about how to understand themselves and how to see beyond, or let go of, all the noise that surrounds every waking minute.

This married with a general education that includes personal well being, covering such areas as how to get better sleep at night, how to eat healthily, how to be a true friend, how to communicate, how to relieve your own stress, how to learn, where to go for information and who you can trust, must be the way forward for the next generation to survive this assault on their psychological equilibrium.

When two people meet

Whenever two people meet there are really six people present. There is each person as they see themselves, each person as the other person sees them, and each person as they really are.

Life as a mirror

Taking your *Life CV* from *The South* section, look at the ailments, traumas, major problems or dramas you have had in your life. If you think of more then don't forget to add them to your *Life CV*. Can you find positives that have come from each one of them? What has the issue, event or person taught you about yourself?

This mirroring is a common theme in spiritual work. What you give out, will come back to you. Negative thoughts and words sent out to another person, for example, may return to bite you, in one way or another. In fact just being in a negative space can have a detrimental effect on your day. We have all experienced this when, for example, we wake up in a bad mood (maybe due to something that happened the day or night before), stub our toe, spill the coffee, burn the toast, are stuck in traffic and subsequently late for work, have an argument with a colleague, forget to pick up the dry cleaning, etc., and eventually write it off as a bad day.

Conversely a positive start to the day can keep us energised and allow (or maybe create) a good day to follow. A morning meditation, prayer, affirmation or a general positive outlook when we first awaken, even just by saying hello to the world, can help kick start the day, and, if practised regularly, can lead to longer periods of good days, resulting in a more stable, clearer and calmer emotional state overall.

Dropping the ego to allow space for creation

Out thoughts create our reality. If we are in a negative mood then what we are likely to create will reflect this. Conversely if we can be peaceful, content, and in balance when we go about our day, the creation impulses will be more positive. What often drives this negative or positive tug of war is our ego. That part of us that wants to be in control, knows what is best and what is right according to *the law of us*.

The ego is clearly influenced by many factors and shaped from an early age, continuing to be our core self until we do something about it. If we don't then the ability to see things differently, to embrace empathy, and understand another's point of view diminishes, and we only take on board, seek out or connect with, what feeds our ego; that which we already agree with. Anything outside of this is dismissed. Some call it character, or personality which is fine, but where is the space for change? How does one go about it?

Below are some ways to shatter your ego given by Daniel Whalen, NLP Master Practitioner:[14]

- Kill the addiction to approval.
- Seek out praise for others.
- Let go of the false power of anger.
- Spend time alone in nature.
- Be still.
- Use irritation from others as a mirror for yourself.
- Give in to vulnerability.

---

[14] *13 Little But Powerful Ways To Shatter Your Ego,* Daniel Whalen, *Neuro-Linguistic Programming (NLP) Master Practitioner, Thoughtcatalog.com,* 7/6/2018.

- Suppress the need to add your opinion to everything
- Question why you do what you do.
- Locate yourself in others as often as possible.

Many of the exercises within this book have been about looking inwards and reflecting on our nature. In a way this is holding a mirror up to your ego and asking is this truly who I am, or who I want to be?

Other ways to reduce the ego effect are:

- Be in the flow. Do things you love.
- Practice meditation and mindfulness.
- Feel gratitude and compassion. Use your gratitude stones.
- Embrace childhood innocence. Nurture your inner child.
- Foster humility. Go on a pilgrimage, to a religious site or a natural one.

Ikigai : Your reason for being

Ikigai is a Japanese concept relating to one's reason for living, and can be seen as the convergence of four primary elements:

What you Love (your passion)
What you are Good at (your vocation)
What the World Needs (your mission)
What you can get Paid for (your profession)

Draw your own version of the overlapping circles of the *ikigai* symbol below and consider the following:

- *What do you love?* What aspects of your life bring you into your heart and make you come alive?

- *What are you good at?* What unique skills do you have that come most naturally to you? What talents have you cultivated and what do you excel at, even when you aren't trying? What is your medicine?

- *What cause do you believe in?* What breaks your heart or pulls at your gut? What change would you most love to create in the world? What would you give your life for?

- *What do people value and pay you for?* What service, value or offering do you bring, or could you bring, that is of real value to others? Something people need and are happy to pay for or share some value in exchange?

Write whatever key words, phrases and ideas come up for you in each circle, then look for areas of natural overlap. Are any of these elements related to each other? The space in the middle is where your *ikigai* resides. Spend time contemplating or meditating as to what this could be. Is there one thing you could do that would help this expression of your *ikigai*?

Vision or dream board

Create a collage of your dreams and wishes using glossy magazine pictures, photos, newspaper images, or any picture or symbol that represents what you want from life. Arrange these on a board, ensuring the images are connected, touching each other or overlapping. Keep it in a prominent place so that you see it every day, looking at the images and visualising your dreams in a slightly more tangible way. Take a photo of the vision board with your phone so you can gaze upon it wherever you are.

Look for any linkages or themes in the pictures. What is this vision telling you about yourself? Is this really you, or are you just wishing from a place of lack? Desiring something you believe you should have, or you have been told you should desire? For example a steady job, long term relationship, three bed house, two children, nice car, etc. These may well be true for you but allow yourself total freedom to dream as wildly and grandly, or as specifically and humbly as you wish. Update the board regularly as your dreams change or evolve.

Dream journal

Keep a journal by your bed, or use the voice recorder function on your phone, to record your dreams. This is easier said than done as they can often disappear in a moment once we begin to awaken. The trick is to stay with the dream once you have come out of it. Not moving or opening the eyes and taking time to review the dream, crystallising the main points in the now semi-awake mind, before making the conscious effort to awake fully and record the dream.

It has been said that dreams are a method by which the soul is trying to talk to us, or maybe just the sub-conscious. Maybe they are similar or the same. The language though can be difficult to interpret and the metaphors not obvious. Look for patterns in dreams, especially ones that repeat, but take the explanations for dreams available in books or the internet with a pinch of salt. Use your own discernment to understand any meaning.

Affirmations

An affirmation is the reciting of inspirational and aspirational words that resonate with you. It is a positive reinforcement of who you are and who you want to be. Your own mantra. It should be written by yourself, making it personal and pertinent. Use positive, expansive, self-affirming, or energising words.

Write the affirmation as though it is your truth, and how you currently behave, even if you feel you do not openly show these behaviours. Write it with confidence. Do not use doubtful wording like "maybe", "if", "I hope that...", etc. Use statements, such as "I am", "I know", or "It is". It may seem like an essay first time round, but once you have the outline, refine it. Edit it down to a core powerful affirmation. Write out your affirmation clearly, maybe with an artistic flare by adding colour, using calligraphic swirls or even adding pictures. Keep it out in the open and read it every day, in the morning and evening. Read it out loud, saying it to yourself in a mirror. Look into your eyes and believe what you are saying. If there is doubt or you feel silly or stupid, look at the reason why? Are these just not your words? Does something not feel right? If the affirmation is reasonable then often it is something within us that is the issue. Look at the reason for this block, using one of the exercises from previous chapters to unearth and transmute it. A quick online search will throw up many affirmation examples, but a few are given here:

> *"I surrender to all life has to offer and I am excited by the adventure that lies ahead. I am confident in my abilities and trust I will be helped and supported through all my endeavours. I know how to make decisions and am ready to deepen my relationships with spirit and the Universe."*

> *"I am an intelligent, caring and empathic woman, confident in my abilities, happily independent and compassionate to all I meet. I know how beautiful I am and how much love is in my heart."*

Or from Sue Stone's book *Love Life, Live Life:*[15]

> *"I trust in the power and magic of the Universe.*
> *I believe in miracles, miracles happen to me.*
> *I have more love, happiness and abundance in my life than I ever imagined possible."*

Take a photo of what you have written on your phone and refer to it throughout the day, leaving the original in a prominent place in your home. You could use your symbol (see the *create your symbol* exercise) or carry a talisman as a reminder of this affirmation.

---

[15] Sue Stone, *Love Life, Live Life, 2010, Piatkus.*

Pioneer / frontier spirit

One does not have to be physically exploring new places, clambering up mountains or diving to the depths of the oceans to be a pioneer, as every person alive right now is standing at the forefront of human evolution. 99.9% of species that have ever existed are now extinct, but humans have survived (and evolved) to be here at this moment in time. We are breathing rarefied air, even if society and the media machine continues to churn away, seemingly treating us as sheep and keeping us asleep spiritually.

We can however, if we chose to, embrace this pioneer spirit. What frontiers do you want to push? What knowledge has been hidden from you? What nagging doubts do you have around life as you see it, or how it has been presented to you? What doesn't sit right or seem to fit? What cultures, other than your own, can you learn from? What wisdom is out there awaiting you? What piece (or pieces) of the jigsaw are missing for you?

Yes it is simpler and, arguably, easier to follow the herd, to go along with what society expects, but why not go a little outside of your comfort zone, go where there is resistance. Face the fear and do it anyway! (see *Move out of your comfort zone* in *The West* section).

Exploring exercise

When in a new place geographically, maybe on holiday or a day trip, you are unfamiliar with the area and do not know your way around, so you need to go out and explore. The first time you venture out on foot in this new place a strong focus is kept on remembering the way back. You look around of course, but always with one eye on the return journey, and therefore probably don't take everything in. On the second outing the route is known and time can be taken to really look around. The third time out you can try another route, confident that you know the area well enough to find your way back. With phones and GPS the chances of getting lost are slim, but even though this is not in the jungle, on a mountain, or deep under the sea, this is still exploring.

This sense of exploring can be translated to spiritual exercises. Wariness and insecurity on the first attempt of an exercise, understanding on the second, and confidence then after, whenever the exercise is practised. This is one of the many reasons why a journal is important; to go back and revisit your notes and the exercises undertaken, and then see if you can go *off map* a little.

And speaking of maps, the maps we are most familiar with provide us with a detailed scaled overview of the land, containing symbols and graphical representations of the real world to help us navigate on a journey. A map provides a bigger picture. Normally an overhead view, looking down on the area. It can be used to get from one place to another, but can give much more information than just a route. Geographical features are normally shown, such as green spaces, rivers, coastline, forests and contour lines to show hills and valleys. Places of interest are often marked on maps and can be included as stop offs during a journey. Seeing an overall picture of the area may throw up new ideas on where to go, or how to take a different route to include a visit to the coast, cross a particular river or pass through a local village for lunch.

Such geographical and road maps are two types of map but there are many others, such as weather, historical, time zone, habitat, population, climate, political, economic, resource, tourist, nautical, the night sky, or even a map of the brain and the neural hotspots within, all giving a bigger picture of what is happening and how the individual parts connect and relate to the whole. Then there are mind maps to organise information, so that linkages between sometimes disparate subjects can be revealed. With the advent of GPS tracking real time maps can show the movements of tagged animals, traffic congestion and, more subversively, the movement people carrying mobile phones, which nowadays is almost everyone.

When journeying or meditating we often go to the same or similar places in our minds, places that feel safe, powerful or where we meet spiritual allies or helpers. Mapping this inner landscape may prove useful in understanding our own psyche. A couple of the exercises in this book are also ways of producing personal maps to some degree, namely mapping your past in the *Life CV* exercise or mapping your dreams with a vision board.

The process of producing a map is a wonderful learning tool and exploratory in nature, in and of itself. Modern technology has however detracted from this sense of exploring when it comes to going to new places. There are those that will happily venture out even if unsure of where they are and confidently get lost, knowing that they will be able to get back using their phone. Mobile phones have taken away the need to observe and take in our surroundings, as wherever we are, our position can be pinpointed on a digital map, and a taxi, or similar, requested to take us home. Being overly reliant upon technology has taken us a little further from our connection to nature and, in this case, traditional ways of navigating and exploring. It worth trying to get lost, just once in a while, to rekindle that pioneer and explorer feeling within.

Mother Earth - Our relationship to the environment and all life on this planet

"Now is the time to give back to Pacha Mama, Mother Earth. Now is the time for reconnecting to her."
Message from the Q'ero people.

Connection has been referred to often in this book, and there is none more profound than our connection to the planet we live upon and the life we share it with. This is our home, and currently our only home. It is not part of this book's remit to go into the issues of climate change, species extinction, habitat loss, population growth, food quality, clean air and water, or other environmental challenges but they are clearly problems that we all are facing in one way or another.

However, I would say that the two most important factors over the coming years will be **transparency** and **sustainability** in all we do as a species, at every level of society. If all our endeavours, individually, corporately, governmentally, and culturally, are sustainable from the point of view of resource use and environmental impact, and all companies and governments are open and honest, then the crisis we are faced with may be surmounted.

It will take visionary and revolutionary individuals; leaders, creators and developers in all walks of life, to move our culture forward to where the future, for us and our childrens' children, looks bright. We should have faith in people, in young people especially. If they are offered the right education, the right tools to apply to problems, and the chance to use their own creative abilities, then change, and a new future, is within our grasp.

The Earth is in a constant state of flux, of death and rebirth, of mutation and transformation. Nothing is static. Convection currents, in the molten iron outer core at the heart of the planet, generate a global magnetic field, shaped by the Earth's rotation. This magnetic field protects us from harmful solar radiation and provides animals with an evolved sensory capability, a map by which to navigate through their daily lives, or guide them on an annual migration of many hundreds or even thousands of miles.

The ebb and flow of the oceans, the warming and cooling of land and water, the movement of air, cloud formation and weather systems; all is in a continual state of change and yet we, as sentient conscious mammals, struggle with change. We can become set in our ways, creatures of habit, comfortable with the familiar, fearful of the unknown, the strange and different. Change is seen as a challenge rather than the natural occurrence it is.

If we take time to look at the Earth, and become aware of the abundance and number of different environments, we are left in awe at the magnificence and beauty of our planet and the staggering variety and diversity that thrives upon her. But we soon forget, especially when so much time is spent within the same few groups of four walled boxes (home, school or work), looking at one rectangular screen or another, staring out at other rectangular boxes, some towering high in the sky blocking out the natural light, or even laying on a rectangular bed staring up at rectangular ceiling, perhaps in expectation of inspiration and a deeper understanding of who we are and why we are here. It must be difficult to see beyond our compartmentalised lives at times, to see the wonder of nature, the beauty of life and the miracles that occur constantly. Miracles that are in fact just natural happenings, things that mother nature has been doing for hundreds, thousands, and maybe millions of years.

So to help ourselves we need to ensure our connection to the planet remains strong, or if it has become diminished, is reignited and reinforced. The fears and misnomers about nature and man's relationship to nature; how we must master it, overcome it, defeat it; must be seen as the fearful, indoctrinated views of a time long since past.

Those that live, and have lived, in harmony with nature, not only indigenous peoples but also those who work daily on the land as part of their livelihood, coupled with the increasing number of people who are choosing to go back to nature in one way or another, accept that they are part of natural landscape. They understand that nature is not to be bent to their will, but a partner to be understood, respected and cherished, and as such, worked with, not against. They know that we are in stewardship of the land, not ownership. We should be looking after it for those who will come after us.

One does not have to go off grid or become a sustainable farmer to develop this natural relationship. There are simple things anyone can do to rekindle this connection with Mother Nature, such as keeping house plants, or herbs on the windowsill, composting organic waste, growing your own fruit and veg, re-purpose your outdoor spaces to attract insects and birds, or provide food and water for animals. Also improving your home's energy efficiency, being conscious of the food you buy and eat, and reducing the amount of water wasted are beneficial to a more sustainable lifestyle. Again there are a myriad of books and online content on sustainable, natural living, and the positive effects it can have on your wellbeing and the life you lead if you wish to learn more.

It is my belief that we, as humans, have the energies of the planet at our disposal. The animals and plants, the waterways and air, the soil and land, all available to us to use, to commune with and work with in a spiritual way, to help ourselves understand and strengthen this primeval connection. The medicine plants, ancient trees, flowing waterfalls, rocks, crystals, and every other natural resource, all can have a significance for us on our journey through life and play their part in forming our internal, as well as external, landscape.

Plant medicines

The term plant medicine is used to cover all products produced from plants to treat disease, or help with health. In this section I am only referring to the psychoactive plants used in shamanic cultures for healing work. To the majority of westerners these types of plant medicines are purely 'drugs' and, if illegal, to be avoided, deemed dangerous, and anyone who takes or *uses* them condemned. These are not plant medicines. These are recreational drugs, perhaps experimented with initially when an adolescent and sometimes used more regularly in adulthood, often as an escape. Yes there can be progression onto more potent and addictive substances, possibly resulting in wrecked lives and even death, but this is not the inevitable path for most who try recreational drugs. Of course, legal drugs such as tobacco and alcohol are deemed acceptable by society, even though they cause more harm than probably any other form of either legal or illegal recreational drug.

All medicines have come from nature originally. Their active ingredients isolated from the plant, fungi, tree, or other organic matter in a lab, and then chemically replicated so that the medicine can be mass produced, in pill or potion form. No doubt, for the majority of people, prescribed medication has helped. But this is too often only a way to treat the symptoms and not the underlying cause.

Prescribed drugs also have side effects, some physical but also some psychological, and possibly affecting mental health. For example, often cited side effects of anti-depressants are an emotional numbing of the patient and the associated feeling of being detached from life.

The healing effect of plant medicines is beginning to be recognised by western medicine, with continuing research being conducted by various respected bodies including the Psychedelic Trials Group, King's College London, and the Centre for Psychedelic Research, Imperial College London, who have promising results from a recent trial using psilocybin (the active ingredient in magic mushrooms) to help treat clinical depression.[16]

From a shamanic perspective, plant medicines are gifts from *Mother Earth* and are cultivated and prepared by the shaman or shamanic practitioner in a sacred way, the spirit of the plant honoured and the potent healing properties respected. When plant medicines are used it is within the framework of a ceremony and not recreationally, often with days or weeks of preparation by the individual beforehand, possibly including abstinence from alcohol, sex and drugs, eating a natural and cleansing diet, or spending time in meditation readying oneself.

Plant medicines are an important part of shamanic and indigenous cultures and a vibrant natural way to connect to non-ordinary reality, whilst also affording a method to supercharge your imagination and *see* in your mind, especially helpful if you find visualising difficult.

Personally I do not feel that plant medicines are necessary to live a spiritual life, but if you are going to venture deeper into shamanism or nature based spirituality they will be encountered and, quite naturally, one would want to experience their potent effects.

---

[16] David Nutt, David Erritzoe, Robin Carhart-Harris, *Psychedelic Psychiatry's Brave New World*, Cell volume 181 Issue 1, 02/04/2020.

However, I strongly suggest that plant medicines should not be used as a direct *go to* for spiritual enlightenment, or a vacation add on, rather used only after a period of working on yourself (such as via the exercises in this book for example), so that you have uncovered and possibly cleared many of your blocks or issues beforehand.

Note: Safety warning
If you choose to take plant medicines you need to be aware of their legality, which varies from country to country, and I strongly suggest only taking them in a formalised ceremony, under the guidance of a qualified shaman or shamanic practitioner you trust (and have known long enough to build trust with), in a place, and with a group where you feel safe and secure.

Working with plant medicines can be traumatic if you do not know what you are doing, so you need to place your trust totally in those that are conducting the ceremony.

There will always be negative stories around such activities but the vast majority of shaman and shamanic practitioners honour the sacredness of the work they have been called to undertake and hold safe, loving ceremonies to help heal their communities.

General connecting and balancing visualisation

When out in nature take a moment to stop and, either standing or sitting, close your eyes and breathe in the life force that is all around. Slow down and connect with the sounds and smells and let the energy of the space you are in flow in and out with your breath. Feel alive with all your senses.

Taking this further, the next visualisation can act as a way to connect you to all there is, and help clear blockages and fill gaps from any perceived loss, bringing you back into a healthy balance.

All life came from the stars. Atoms of matter created during, or soon after the Big Bang, have formed and reformed over billions of years, been transformed and transmuted in generation after generation of star formation, recycled and redistributed when the stars turn supernova and explode. After more than a thousand generations of these stellar formations our star, the Sun, was birthed (about 4.6 billion years ago) and the Solar System, including Earth, subsequently coalesced into being.

Over time the atmosphere, land and seas formed on our planet, with the first life appearing around three billion years ago. The heat, light and invisible (to humans) electromagnetic radiation produced by the Sun fuelled the development of the first organisms and continues to be the building block of all life on Earth. We are connected to everything through this process of stellar evolution. Connected to all that has been, and all that will be, by the Sun.

Relax and allow your breathing to slow. Ideally be outside on a sunny day where you can safely feel the Sun on your face, otherwise imagine the Sun's rays beaming down upon you. Begin by focusing on the Sun in your mind. Travel out in space and be in front of it. Feel, as best you can, it's enormity and power. Let it blast through you, vaporise you, dismantle you totally, annihilate every molecule, every atom. Then allow the disintegrated mist that is *you* to drift through space to Earth, and be scattered across the whole planet. Feel as though *you* covers the planet, becoming part of the water in the oceans, evaporating into clouds, falling as rain, into lakes, streams and rivers and flowing back to the sea. Feel yourself mingle with the atmosphere and become the air every plant and leaf takes in, the air every animal and human breathes. Breathe in knowing you are linked to everything, breathe out knowing whatever has left you goes to connect with everything outside of you. Continue to bring the inner and outer into balance. Everything is in you, you are in everything. Visualise your energy body and allow blockages to dissipate, voids to be filled. Repeat the mantra "I am one with the Universe, the Universe is one with me", or "I am one with God (or spirit), God (or spirit) is one with me". Find balance in this cycle of breathing everything in and out.

Note: The number of atoms in the human body is 7 octillion $(7x10^{27}$ - a seven with twenty seven zeros after it). Planet Earth is 510 trillion $(510x10^{12})$ square metres in total surface area (land and sea), so if your body was vaporised into a wind of atoms that were scattered upon the whole of the earth's surface, then the maths works out at around 13 trillion $(13x10^{12})$ atoms of *you* per square metre, which clearly means there would be a vast part of *you* everywhere, and *you* would most definitely be part of everything. If you replace atoms for the much larger human cell in which they reside (and containing the building block of life, DNA), then this still works out at around a dozen cells per square metre across the whole surface of the planet. Knowing this may help with the visualisation.

Strip away exercise

Remove from your mind everything man made on this planet, just as an exercise. I am not saying live in the past, just go back there in your mind. Pre-industrial revolution. Just humans and nature in a simple symbiotic, bountiful and peaceful relationship. For this exercise ignore thoughts around any difficulties living, disease, famine, natural disasters, etc. Visualise only living in peace. Living comfortably off the land and being content. Visualise the Moon, stars, seas, tides, cycles of nature, from trees fruiting to animal migrations. Remember how simple it was to live with the resources around us. Having the teachings of how to do this passed on from generation to generation. Connect again with the energy of these teachings, a wisdom based in nature. Now bring these healthy, content, symbiotic living feelings, back to your current life. Feel how they are still prevalent and pertinent in this world with all its technology, gadgets, systems and man-made constructions. See how this knowledge still has value and is available if we work with our natural state and create space for it. This natural connection can soon be rekindled by spending time in nature, away from the frenetic activity of the city and urban life.

Trees and wood

Trees have naturally been mentioned many times in this book, which is unsurprising knowing their value to the natural world, and to us as humans. But their significance can only be touched upon in these pages as their usefulness is seemingly unending, as providers of oxygen, fire for warmth, security and cooking, building materials, food, medicines, rubber, incense and resins, to play upon as children, shelter under out of the rain, doze against in the shade on a summer's afternoon, or even climb up into out of a predator's reach! Wood can be carved into bowls and spoons, made into furniture, artwork or toys, transformed into paper and books, used to make tools, arrows or spears, or simply used as a walking stick. It is no surprise that trees, and the wood they provide, are so revered.

It is not only for practical reasons that the tree is so loved. Spiritually too it plays its role. The tree has always been linked to spiritual metaphor; growing tall and strong from a small seed, anchoring roots deep into the earth and spreading its bows heavenwards, exchanging carbon dioxide for oxygen (and, in the case of the oak, looking almost like the brachia of human lungs). This above and below metaphor, the duality of life, is encapsulated in the tree. From the outset we as humans are split into male and female. Half the world population is women, half men. Duality is a given, night and day, on and off, left and right, up and down, male and female, as above, as below. Why then should it be any different when it comes to a spiritual outlook on life? This duality persists. In the form of an upward, or above, higher spiritual connection, coupled with a downward, or lower, deeper soul connection. As Bill Plotkin highlights in his book *Soulcraft:*[17]

> *"Spirit connection above, soul purpose below.... Soul embraces and calls us toward what is most unique in us. Spirit encompasses and draws us toward what is most universal and shared."*

Reaching for the sky whilst being rooted to the earth, trees show us both the above and the below coming together in one - a wonderful representation of the human spiritual journey. Sending roots down in discovery of the soul, creating a strong foundation for the trunk of core growth, that in turn supports the desire to extend upwards and to connect to what is beyond, to what is out of reach; even perhaps to all that is.

This symbolism, married with the evident natural connection, is the reason the tree is often used for shamanic or spiritual journeying work as the *axis mundi* for spiritual exploration; to embark on a lower world journey via the roots or hollow in the tree taking us down, or climbing the trunk and branches skywards to help send us towards the upper world.

---

[17] Bill Plotkin, *Soulcraft*, 2003, New World Library.

With all its uses, in particular as a building material for shelter, and fuel for heating and cooking, wood was historically seen as being more than just useful but essential. Not having wood to cook with or warm a shelter would clearly be a disastrous situation, whilst conversely having an abundance of wood could be seen as fortunate, perhaps even lucky to some degree. Knocking on wood or using the phrase "touch wood" reflects this. Moreover, the feel of wood, by hugging a tree, sitting at a wooden table, or holding a stick, is grounding; it provides that feeling of connection to something natural and to Mother Nature in general. Compare holding something wooden to something plastic, for example.

There is also the artistic element of wood that gives it value; the colour, shapes, textures and patterns created by the grain, and the way it wears over time, its patina, revealing a history of use and often becoming more visually beautiful with age.

Try cultivating your relationship with trees and wood. What trees do you know? Which ones are native to your country or area? Make your own staff or walking stick, use wood in your hobbies; carve a spoon, make a spice rack or bird box. Make a conscious effort to touch and feel anything wooden. Choose wood over man made materials in your home for your furniture, especially tables. Reclaim, restore and re-purpose wooden items. Touch and feel the bark of a tree. Say hello to a tree, even give one a hug. Wander your neighbourhood and take in all the trees around you. Spot the tallest or largest tree in a group. This, research is now discovering, is often the grandmother tree that looks after all those under her care, by communicating via her roots with the underground fungal network, and sending out water and nutrients, to help any local tree in distress.

The 2019 study, *Protect Oak Ecosytems*[18], (sadly started in response to an acute decline of oak trees within the UK) showed that native oaks are home to some 2,300 separate species, with over five hundred completely dependent, or highly reliant upon the oak. So next time you look at an oak realise that it is more than just a tree, but actually a whole ecosystem of lifeforms living together and calling the tree their home.

Trees have stood through the centuries, survived lightning strikes and disease, and grown to be one of the largest living organisms on earth. General Sherman, a Giant Sequoia, in the Sequoia National Park, California, USA, is approximately 2,500 years old and thought to weigh in the region of 2,000 tonnes. The national park is full of these incredible trees and a hike in the area feels truly like walking amongst giants. California must be a good climate for trees, as nearby in the White Mountains is a bristle cone pine that is believed to be the oldest living organism on the planet, at approximately 5,000 years old.

Trees, and the forests they thrive within, have been stable havens for the natural world for much longer than a few thousand years. In fact rainforests are the oldest eco-systems on Earth. Some can trace their origins back to 70 million years ago, when dinosaurs roamed the planet, with the rainforest of Borneo thought to be around a staggering 130 million years old.

If trees could speak, what stories they would tell. They rightly have a special place in our hearts and we must do all we can to ensure future generations will reap their benefits.

---

[18] Their website: protectouroaks.wordpress.com

Create your own talking stick or wand

A talking stick is sometimes used in group settings, when sat in council or sharing. It is passed around the group and signifies whose turn it is to speak, while all others listen in silence. It gives the holder permission, and the authority, to compose themselves, speak from the heart, and take their time saying what they want to say, without fear of interruption. Using a wooden stick provides something natural and tangible to hold whilst collecting thoughts, and can be a focal point if words are struggling to be spoken. It can be held loosely and gesticulated with when in full flow, or held tightly and squeezed if deeper emotion comes with what has to be said. Passing the stick around the group (normally sat in a circle) gives a chance for every person present to speak, and not only the loudest or most self confident. All can, and should be heard, as everybody has some wisdom to share.

This, I believe, is part of the origin of wands. We look at magic, the occult, witches and wizards, with much scepticism in the modern world. But take yourself back to a time when we were living in a far deeper connection to the land, and trees, and the wood they provided, were honoured as the wonderful resource they were. It is then not too difficult to comprehend the development of such magical sticks.

So try making your own talking stick or wand by finding a piece of wood that is about 30cms (12 inches) in length that feels right in your hand. Ensure it is strong enough to withstand being held tightly and resist being bent or snapped. Trim and carve it with a knife, removing any shoots, bumps or ridges along the length of the stick, leaving enough texture as is your personal preference (but avoiding splinters), and ensuring there are no sharp edges or prongs on the ends.

You can use this stick in ceremonial work, just to hold and feel the natural connection, or as your own personal talking stick, to wave as a wand, draw on the ground in the dirt or leaf litter, or to tap on various parts of your body to help emotional release. Keeping it on or near your altar will help reinforce it's potency and usefulness.

Be a tree

Ideally do this exercise on the earth with bare feet but, if not possible, just visualise yourself stood on the land.

Stand and imagine roots coming out from the soles of your feet. Allow these roots to spread and go deep into the earth, visualising them twisting and turning their way through the soil and into the rock, maybe through air pockets or caves deep below. Then extend your arms out and up, as the branches of a tree, and look skywards. Breathe in and visualise sunlight and heavenly energy entering you through your hands, arms and face, moving down through your torso, and then as you breathe out send this energy through your torso and legs, out of your feet and through your roots into the earth. Maybe *see* the energy as a colour. Then reverse the process. This time, on the in breath, bring life force energy up from the earth, through your roots, into your feet and up into your entire body. Then, on the out breath, see it flow out of your head and outstretched arms into the Universe. Repeat this cycle, flushing yourself with alternate Universe and Earth energy, until you feel cleansed, recharged and balanced.

Some tai-chi, qi-gong and yoga movements are based on this tree symbolism and metaphor.

Sit under a tree

Trees can act as antennas. They were used as such in the Vietnam war, and since by electronics hobbyists. But they can also be spiritual antennas, allowing us to commune with nature and our inner selves. The Buddha is said to have achieved enlightenment whilst sat under a bodhi (fig) tree whilst in meditation. So why not try this for yourself? Sit under a tree with your back to the trunk, and connect with the tree. Ask it a question. Close your eyes or let your gaze soften and drift, allowing the answer to come to you, either in your imagination or as a message from nature, such as an animal coming into view, a sound, or even words from a conversation between people passing by.

The plaque on the bench my father made in memory of my mother, who passed in 1998, says "To be close to me, just sit by a tree."

Belly button stick

The belly button, or navel, is the attachment point for the umbilical chord, through which, whilst in the womb, we received the energy and nutrients necessary to grow from our mother, via the placenta. Revisit this connection by taking a small stick about two centimetres (one inch) in diameter and holding it into, or onto, your belly button, whilst tapping it rhythmically with another stick. Feel the vibration and bring your focus to your mother. What emotions or feelings come up doing this?

Try using a longer stick to connect your belly button directly to the earth. Tap this longer stick. Again feel the vibration and dwell on the connection being made to *Mother Earth.*

Fungi

Fungi are not part of the plant or animal kingdoms. In fact, they have their own classification and are a kingdom of their own. There is much more to these organisms than perhaps first thought. We now know that we only see the fruiting part of the fungus on the surface, whilst the main body, the mycelium, lies hidden underground and forms part of an underground communication network, a *wood-wide-web*, between many, if not all, of the local plants and trees with roots in the soil.

Richard Gray's article, *The Unexpected Magic of Mushrooms*[19], highlights more astonishing facts, some of which are summarised below:

> *"Fungi are some of the most common organisms on our planet; the combined biomass of these often tiny organisms exceeds that of all the animals on the planet put together. And we are discovering new fungi all the time. More than 90% of the estimated 3.8 million fungi in the world are currently unknown to science. In 2017 alone, there were 2,189 new species of fungi described by scientists.*
>
> *A recent report published by the UK's Royal Botanic Gardens in Kew, London, highlighted that fungi are already used in hundreds of different ways, from making paper to helping to clean our dirty clothes.*
>
> *Around 15% of all vaccines and biologically produced drugs come from fungi. The complex proteins used to trigger an immune response to the hepatitis B virus, for example, are grown in yeast cells, which are part of the fungi family.*

---

[19] Richard Gray, *The Unexpected Magic of Mushrooms*, 15/03/19, *BBC future* website.

Perhaps the most well-known is the antibiotic penicillin, which was discovered in a common type of household mould that often grows on old bread. Dozens of other types of antibiotics are now produced by fungi...

...A fungus found growing in soil at a landfill site on the outskirts of Islamabad, Pakistan, may be a solution to the alarming levels of plastic pollution clogging up our oceans. Fariha Hasan, a microbiologist at Quaid-I-Azam University in Islamabad, discovered the fungi Aspergillus tubingensis can rapidly break down polyurethane plastic...
...California-based MycoWorks have been developing ways of turning mushrooms into building materials. By fusing wood together with mycelium, they have been able to create bricks that are fire-retardant and tougher than conventional concrete...

...Fungi can also be used in combination with traditional building materials to create a "smart concrete" that can heal itself as the fungi grows into any cracks that form, secreting fresh calcium carbonate, the key raw material in concrete, to repair the damage."

Clearly, our knowledge of these mainly hidden organisms is still in its infancy, with more uses undoubtedly waiting to be unearthed.

Holding history

History is often pieced together from small pieces of evidence; shards of bone, broken artefacts, fossilised remains. These pieces tell a story if one knows how to read them. However you do not need to be a historian or an archaeologist to connect to the past. We can all do this easily, not only by meditation, visualisation or journeying, but by connecting with nature, especially ancient natural objects such as the rocks and stones formed many millions of years ago. In the UK the youngest are about 50 million years old, the oldest 500 million. Scientists in North America have found rocks believed to be over four billion years old, in Hudson Bay, Northern Quebec.

So touching a rock face, sitting on a boulder, picking up a pebble from the beach or holding a crystal, is a direct link to the past. Choose a stone you like, maybe one that has special meaning to you and sit with it. Look at it, feel it's history. Notice how it has weathered, been eroded over time, or possibly broken off from a much larger piece. If you are in the UK, accept that it is at least 50 million years old. Can you begin to imagine that sort of time? Holding a fossil can have a similar effect, perhaps more so than a rock, as you are holding something that was alive millions of years ago.

When out walking, if you see a fern, stop for moment and realise that it comes from one of the oldest groups of plants still alive today, dating all the way back to the Devonian period, 400 million years ago. A living fossil. Another is the gingko tree. This species of tree has survived since before the age of the dinosaurs, with fossilised leaves discovered, dating back more than 200 million years, that are almost the same as they now.

Some animals too have changed little over time and are classed as living fossils. The horseshoe crab, crocodile, elephant shrew, spectacled bear, giant salamander and the infamous coelacanth fish to name just a few. Connecting with these animals is a direct link to the past even if it is only through books, TV or the internet. If you are lucky enough to encounter one at a zoo or, more majestically, in the wild, then this connection can be quite humbling.

World water sharing

At a gathering I attended many years ago was a man who had a bottle of liquid he claimed was water from all around the world, that he had been collecting for many years on his travels. He had also asked people he met, or was going to meet, to bring water from their land so that he could add their water to his and vice versa. He shared this water with those at the gathering, so that we all could be part of this wonderfully connecting process.

The mixing and diluting of the water does not detract from this connection as there are so many molecules of water in every drop. In the small 18ml (0.6 fl oz) dropper bottle of water I had there are 6×10^{23} (a six with twenty three zeros after it) molecules of H_2O. So even if the water was diluted one million times there would still be 6×10^{17} molecules of the original water. Therefore I knew the small bottle of water I held, contained a number (a very large number in fact) of molecules from waterways, streams, ponds, rivers, lakes and seas from all over the globe.

Sharing this water by putting a few drops into other's empty bottles (to be topped up with local water) keeps this process alive. Of course, water is in a constant state of flux, moving through a cycle of evaporation and condensing, possibly even freezing, throughout all areas of the globe, and is being mixed up naturally. But I still like this idea of world water sharing; the imparted feeling of connection, and the holding of a small bottle of water that is so meaningful.

Offerings

Offerings to the land, to deities, to spirits, and to departed loved ones, have been given by people throughout history, as an act of remembrance and gratitude. If you feel you wish to make an offering, try and keep it relatively small, as it is the gesture that counts, not the size of the offering. Also ensure it is organic and in-keeping with the environment, not permanent or intrusive. For example, as pretty as they are, tying non biodegradable coloured ribbons to trees is not an offering, rather an egotistical display. The natural world is already so blighted by man's intervention and constructions that we should endeavour not to add to this problem.

Nature mandala

When out on the land create a beautiful mandala, or picture, out of the natural objects nearby. Choose somewhere that feels right for you or where you notice objects that you feel you want to touch and arrange in some way. Some people like to balance rocks on the beach, others adorn trees with iconography and messages. Please make sure whatever you use is natural and biodegradable. Open space beforehand if you are drawn to and create a circle with natural objects such as, leaves, feathers, stones or twigs. Perhaps place an object on the four cardinal directions and decorate the surrounds as you see fit. Create something beautiful and meaningful to you, in tune with the landscape. Have an intention as you create it, even if it is just a thank you to *Mother Earth*.

The elements

The four elements of earth, air, fire and water (and sometimes a fifth, metal or aether) have been honoured and respected by all cultures as being the basic elements of our planet, pre-dating any scientific knowledge around the periodic table. Nowadays, of course, we realise this is a simplistic view due to the complexity of the chemistry at play. Nonetheless revering and working spiritually with these basic elements can still offer insight and tangible benefits. We encapsulate the elements within ourselves; fire as temperature, water as blood, earth as bones, and air in our lungs. We can also look at the elements more esoterically:

- **Earth** - Look to nurture and ground your body: *Feel connected.*

- **Fire** - Burn away the old, stoke the fire of your passions, your hearts calling: *Take action.*

- **Air** - Clear the mind of clutter and negativity, breathe out and let go of what no longer serves you: *Find peace.*

- **Water** - Be in the flow, move with the ebb and tide of your emotions. Take responsibility for how you feel: *Allow movement.*

Throughout this book there are exercises and visualisations that work with the elements either individually or together in some way. Try including objects on your altar that represent the elements, that can be used in meditation or journeying work, and create a nature mandala or artwork honouring each one. Ceremonies can also be created around each of the elements, designed around your own intention. Just keep in mind the general outline of a ceremony; have an intention, open the space, do the spiritual/ceremonial work and end in gratitude before closing the space.

Fire ceremony

The most obvious element to hold a ceremony around is fire. A real fire can clearly become the focal point and central hub for any group work, but can also be worked with individually by building a small fire, or even just using a candle. Often we work with fire at twilight or during the hours of darkness so this lends itself naturally to a more focussed and spiritual connection. Fire is captivating, is seemingly alive in the way the flames dance, the colours morph and glow, the smoke swirls, and the wood crackles, hisses or pops. Additionally, the smell of a wood fire is primordial to a degree, a direct link to the past and all fires that have gone before. Personally I find the smell familiar but mystical, energising but comforting, albeit perhaps less so the next day if still pungent on my clothes. If making a real fire be conscious not to make it too large or waste wood. It should be suited to your or the group's needs.

A fire ceremony can be used for many purposes depending on your intention for it, from welcoming in a new moon phase or season, honouring ancestors or mother nature, letting go and asking the fire to transmute negative or unwanted energies, or as a simple prayer to the fire for something positive to manifest.

Remember to open space before lighting the fire and beginning your ceremony. Write down any prayer, for yourself or another, on a piece of paper, and when the fire is fully lit kneel in front of it and either read out your request or say it again in your head, fully feeling it within yourself. Place the paper into the fire and watch it light and begin to burn before moving away. You may wish to pull the smoke from the fire into your body, into your belly, heart or head, to connect physically to the request you have made. Instead of a piece of paper you could use a stick to hold your prayer, maybe decorating it appropriately beforehand, and feeding it to the fire during the ceremony.

Singing, chanting and drumming whilst around the fire are good ways to raise the energy, and always something I do or encourage with any fire ceremony I attend. Inhibitions can be broken down and the sense of community increased with a shared song. This also acts as a focus for those present when individuals are taking their turn to feed their prayer to the fire. When all have put their paper or stick onto the fire, slowly allow the song/chant/drumming to come to an end and spend a few moment in silence gazing into *Grandfather Fire*. Thank those that have attended, those in spirit that may have been with you and *Grandfather Fire* himself for being with you today and hearing and taking away your prayers. Close the space.

If in a group it is always a good idea to ask everyone to bring food to share after the fire ceremony is over. This is not only a fun group activity but also helps ground the energy from the fire and give people a chance to share with each other. The fire can then be sat around and used as any other camp fire, for toasting marshmallows, sharing a drink, or just softly gazing into.

Natural forces exercises

The forces of nature are breathtaking to behold and often overwhelming with the power they conduct. From lightning storms to volcanic eruptions, tornadoes to earthquakes, tsunamis to wildfires. This power can be tapped into using photos or video footage from the internet for use in your own meditations and journeying work.

This can be taken even further by visualising the most powerful known energies in the Universe, such as the energy emitted from the Sun during a mass coronal ejection event, using footage taken by near sun satellites, or the power of black holes, stars exploding as supernovae, or the biggest bang of them all at the beginning of the Universe.

These are all natural occurrences with mind boggling power and energy associated with them. Why not harness it and use it? If not in reality then in the imaginary. Immerse yourself in this vast energy, knowing you are connected to it.

At the other end of the spectrum the natural world can be used for relaxation, for gentleness and peacefulness. Listen to audio files of the soothing sound of running water, the noise of the wind rustling through the tree tops (psithurism), the gentle background chirp of crickets in warmer climates, or watch nature based mindfulness videos or documentaries to sooth and nourish your soul.

Memorable pets and animal encounters

We have all had pets at some time or another and been drawn to certain animals, even if just in the garden, at the zoo, or when seen on a nature documentary. List out these animals, noting the names of pets, and any other animals you had an affinity with as a child. Are there any animals that you are drawn to now, or keep appearing or popping up at the moment?

Animals are often used in spiritual, and specifically shamanic and animistic settings, as helpers. These power, totem or spirit animals, are called on to come and be with us energetically, to help us and teach us something. Often there is a connection to the animal stemming back to our childhood; maybe it was kept as a pet, we were read stories about it, we saw one regularly in our neighbourhood or had a picture of the animal on our wall.

If you spend time observing animals you will notice that each species has their own particular traits, abilities and behaviours, all of which can show us lessons helpful in our own lives. For example, the team work displayed by a colony of ants is staggering, with each ant seemingly oblivious to any sense of self preservation or selfish behaviour. Everything each ant does is for the colony. There is no moaning or complaining, they just get on and do what nature intended them to do. Altruistic behaviour personified. The patience and stillness of the spider in her web, the acute sight of the hawk, the silence of the owl in flight or the echo location of the bat, all show how wonderfully adapted each of these creatures has become to its own environment. These evolutionary gifts showcase how nature has modified herself over time into the variety and abundance we know today, with the abilities of some within the animal kingdom seemingly magical, as they are so detached from our own capabilities. They are, of course, only natural.

Be an animal

Man has always tried to imitate nature, from singing like a nightingale to dressing up like a peacock, both normally in order to attract a potential mate. In modern times with machinery and technology we can emulate nature further, be it the jaguar's growl heard in the guttural throb of an idling V8 engine, the lion's roar when *roaring* away at speed on a motorbike, or taking to the skies in a plane, para-glider or wing-suit to explore the realm of the birds and soar high over the land and sea.

Shaman work directly with animal spirits, and to help embody the animal further, tribal shaman will often create costumes, head-dresses or jewellery with the animal's feathers, hide or bones. We too can embody the spirit of an animal, with a little dressing up or the applying of make-up to help transform ourselves. If this seems a little extreme then just pretend to be the animal. Be as a child and become the animal. Get on all fours and prowl around like a cat, bark like a dog, howl like a wolf, caw as a crow. Embody this as much as you can, even if you feel uncomfortable.

We all lose our sense of play as we grow older, as expectations and cultural pressures steer us away from childlike innocence and behaviours. Draw on your inner child work from *The North* section and take a few moments to reconnect to the child inside, letting the spirit of the animal you are mimicking take over. Do this for any animal you are drawn to. Maybe start with your power animal if you have met it. Remember that you are not limited to land walking animals. It is only in recent years that we can fly above the clouds and gain the perspective from our airborne cousins point of view. Try flying in your imagination, whilst with arms outstretched as wings, and soar high, then swoop and dive. Or visualise yourself burrowing under the ground, digging into the earth, being surrounded by it, cocooned in *Mother Earth*'s womb. Squeeze through tunnels. Be in your warren, your cave, your chamber. Dive to the depths of the oceans, immersing yourself in the ability to move effortlessly in all directions that being weightless in the water allows.

Play with and explore all of these places in nature, ideally in private, where your inhibitions are lowered, or else you will may attract some interesting and quizzical looks. The use of a blindfold will help keep you in the visualisation.

Mother Earth healing ceremony

This is an outline of a ceremony to honour and offer healing to our planet and all the life she supports. Feel free to adapt it as you wish. If you do not have a specific Mother Earth object on your altar I suggest it is worth finding one. Anything natural that represents nature, a symbolic mother, being nurtured, or similar is fine, as long as it encourages you to think of the planet when you hold it.

Create a nature mandala either outside or within your home, perhaps on or near your altar. Sit next to your natural picture, whilst holding the *Mother Earth* object from your altar, and meditate or journey, sending love and gratitude to the earth. Use a drum, rattle or play an audio file if this helps. Allow your thoughts and the visualisation to become as grand as you can, as powerful as you can. Feel the light of a thousand suns shining out from your heart. See and feel this heart light heal the planet, the wildlife, the forests, rivers and oceans. See it bathe sacred sites, transmute wounds and mend broken relationships. See it bring balance and harmony, and connect to all life. See people as happy, free and alive, ready to fulfil their potential. Love cannot be used up so generate as much as you can. Allow any and all the energy you have transmitted, or channelled to go wherever it is needed and having a positive effect.

When you feel you have done enough, move into gratitude for the gifts you have been given, the gifts you have in return given to the planet, and feel the gratitude and love come back to you from a thankful *Mother Earth*, accepting also that you are worthy to receive such love.

Spend a moment contemplating what actions you can take to continue to help the planet in your normal daily life, even if it is just more reusing, repurposing or recycling.

Father Sky - **Connecting with all that is beyond, the Great Mystery**

"The history of humanity has been slowly increasing the boundaries of knowledge, knowing more and more and more, and feeling comfortable inside there, but at the edges it is always going to be a challenge."
Neil Armstrong.

Above us, in the daytime, are the clouds, birds, the Sun and sky. During the night, the stars, planets and Moon shine, slowly traversing over our heads in their captivating starry firmament way. We look to the heavens for inspiration, throw our hands up into the air in exaltation, in jubilation, and victory. We punch the air when we get a win or a result, in whatever endeavour we are engaged. There is something out of this world (literally) and beyond our reach in the vast space above our heads. Above is far away, untouchable, expansive and aspirational. It is the place of dreams. Quoting Browning again, "Man's reach should exceed his grasp, or what's a heaven for."

It seems to be part of our DNA to explore - to be adventurous and make discoveries. This exploration takes many forms, from navigating upstream on jungle rivers, crossing frozen wastes, diving to the depths of the ocean, rocketing to and stepping upon the lunar surface, or sending probes on infinite journeys into outer space.

These outer explorations are easy to understand and relate to. The planning, expertise and resources necessary for these endeavours, coupled with the bravery (perhaps sometimes foolhardiness) and skills of those undertaking the missions, not only helps provide answers to scientific questions, but offers insights into the human psyche and spirit, reinforcing the belief that we, as a species, can achieve anything we set out to achieve.

Inner explorations and examinations of the small are just as important, but maybe a little more difficult to grasp. Carl Jung suggested a global energetic interconnection when he introduced the term *collective consciousness*, to represent a shared unconscious between all of mankind. Taking this further, the field of quantum is beginning to shed new light on previously held conceptions of reality, linking it with the idea of an energy of consciousness. Physicist, and self proclaimed quantum activist, Dr Amit Goswami, says in his book *The Everything Answer Book:*[20]

> *"Consciousness is the energy behind life, a quantum energy. Thoughts can create things from the quantum of potentiality. This links science and religion or spirituality. The Newtonian scientific view is based around particles and waves being separate. Quantum allows both to exist. It is only when observed that the field collapses and either one or the other is seen."*

Is a quantum energy of consciousness the creation force behind spiritual and energetic healing? Is this how we create our own reality with our thoughts? Maybe such interconnection pervades all life?

Within my shamanic healing work I offer remote sessions, especially useful during the coronavirus pandemic, where the client and I do not have to be in the same room, or even the same country for that matter, as distance is not a barrier to energetic healing, and the powerful transformational effect it can have when a mutual intention is being worked upon.

---

[20] Dr Amit Goswami, *The Everything Answer Book: How Quantum Science Explains Love, Death, and the Meaning of Life*, 2017, Hampton Roads Publishing Co.

Quantum Entanglement, where particles are seemingly connected, even if separated by a distance, is beginning to explain this scientifically, with Einstein calling it, "spooky action at a distance". In my experience, it is not *spooky* but very real, and great changes can take place, even if the practitioner and client are in separate locations.

New scientific discoveries are continually being made, reinforcing the fact that as a species we still have much to learn. At CERN, the international scientific research facility in Switzerland, the Large Hadron Colider (LHCb) is being used to try and unlock some of the mysteries of the Universe and to build upon The Standard Model, that describes all the known fundamental particles that make up the Universe, as well as the forces they interact with. There are new particles being discovered all the time with, in 2018 alone, 59 new hadrons and four tetraquarks added to the list.

Then there is the questions of dark energy and dark matter. What is this energy and matter that is necessary to balance the equations of the observable universe? We are told that the Universe is made up of 85% dark matter. If that is true then how much do we actually know abut the bigger picture of our universe? We clearly do not know it all, and never will we, as science will always lag behind what actually is. As discussed at the beginning of this book, *what is* is *what is*. It is everything. We do not know all the processes, all the procedures, or all the causes and effects. *What is* includes the laws of nature, those we know and have put names and equations to, but also those we currently do not know, or only have loose theories or ideas about.

As I write this the NASA probe New Horizons is flying past Pluto at the outer reaches of our solar system, showing us how far man has come scientifically. Even with such great strides, there are still a myriad of questions waiting to be fully answered by science, such as the previously mentioned question of dark matter and dark energy, the existence of extra-terrestrial life, how to cure illnesses, a better understanding of how the brain works, what is junk DNA for, what is anti-matter, what other exotic energies will the science of quantum throw up to add to The Standard Model? and many, many others.

Science, I'm sure, will eventually provide answers to these questions, or at least lead us towards the answers. Shamanism, and nature based spiritual philosophies, have been able to circumvent the need for answers, as they are a way of life that is inclusive, where it is accepted that we are energetically connected to all life on the planet, and an intrinsic part of an ever changing universe, thus working symbiotically with nature rather than detached from it.

The traditional scientific world view puts man firmly in the middle and separate (often deemed superior) to other lifeforms, which can lead to a blinkered view of *what is*. The Universe, however, is unfolding as it should, in accordance with its own laws, some of which science knows and has labelled, others maybe just glimpsed, or even currently unknown to the scientific community. The parallel paths of science and spirituality are becoming more convergent, with overlaps and cross overs happening more frequently, and perhaps shedding light upon, and connecting us more to, The Great Mystery.

The Sun and Moon

The Sun and Moon have been honoured and worshipped throughout human history, associated with gods and goddesses, surrounded by story and legend, and their motion used to divine prophecy. These two celestial bodies clearly also have a significant effect to life on our planet. The Sun bathes the Earth with its illuminating and warming rays, the energy that drives all life on earth, and an energy we can harness through solar panels as electricity, to power our modern lives. The Sun's path across the sky is an aid for navigation and marks the cycle of the day, with it's colour morphing between golden yellow, orange and red at sunrise and sunset, due to the angle of the light beams through the atmosphere.

The Moon, changing its face each night, as it waxes and wanes, pulling on the tides and all water on the planet, marking cycles of plant growth and female fertility, reflecting down a soft silvery light as a beacon in the darkness of night, and the cosmic coincidence that the moon is exactly the right size for a total eclipse, as although being 400 times smaller than the Sun, it is also 400 times closer to the Earth, all go to make it no surprise that, as the Sun's night-time twin, the Moon is also revered.

Science may tell us the Sun and Moon's composition, their age, their motion within the solar system and path across the sky above, but the influence of these heavenly bodies remains prevalent upon our psyches, as both are also powerful when used in spiritual practices. This is why many annual festivals, celebrations, or ceremonies take place on or around the solar equinoxes and solstices, and no surprise that many ancient constructions were aligned to the Sun, such as Stonehenge and the Great Pyramid at Giza.

The phases of the Moon chart the course of the month and again have always been useful in spiritual practices, with a new moon being a good time for introspection and deciding upon a project or endeavour to embark upon; the waxing moon a time of action to move towards your desired results; the energy and light of a full moon harnessed in rituals and celebrations to savour your labours; before the waning moon signals a period of letting go of that which no longer serves, and finding inherent balance. Personally I find the first and third quarter phases, when the moon if half in shadow, half in light from the Sun, to be a perfect symbol of balance.

So get to know your solar and lunar calendars, there are many apps that can help with this, and maybe look at the cycles of the year with their differing energies, known in the neo-pagan world as sabbats. The eight sabbats of the wheel of the year are:

Imbolc (1st-2nd Feb)   - New beginnings.
Ostara (19-22 Mar)   - Balance of day and night. Spring equinox
Beltane (1st May)   - Growth and abundance.
Litha (19-23 Jun)   - Longest day. The Sun. Summer solstice
Lammas (1st Aug)   - Midsummer.
Mabon (21-24 Sep)   - Harvest. Autumn equinox
Samhain (1st Nov)   - Halloween. All hallows eve.
                        Day of the dead.
Yule (starts 21 Dec) - Shortest day. Midwinter. The Moon.
                        Christmas.

Sun gazing
Note: Safety warning

Never look directly at the Sun. You will do permanent damage to your eyesight.

With eyes closed look in the direction of the Sun and notice the light behind your eyes. Notice how it changes over time. It may begin as yellow but then turn to orange and maybe violet. Fill yourself with this colour, allowing it to seep into every corner of your body, to cleanse and energise. Try this at sunrise or sunset and notice the variation felt between the yellowish colour of the Sun during the day compared to the orange and red of the sunrise or sunset, noticing also the often more peaceful environment at these times of day.

Moon wash

The reflected sunlight from the surface of the Moon is not bright enough to cause damage to your eyes so looking directly at the Moon is quite safe. Ideally on or near a full moon, gaze gently at our natural satellite and breathe in the reflected silvery light, allowing it to flow and shimmer throughout your body, flushing you with silver, and flowing out from your feet into the earth. Bathe in this moonlight allowing it to wash over you completely.

If you have access to a lake or pond try moon washing with both the light directly from the Moon, and that from its reflection in the water, doubling the potency.

The night sky

Who hasn't looked up at the night sky and been in awe. When we do so we are connecting to our ancestors, who looked up just as we have, and felt the same sense of insignificance and wonder. Sadly though, light pollution has taken away this opportunity from many people. In fact, a few years ago, when I was on a stargazing tour in La Palma, one of the Canary Islands, I was informed by the guide that she believed the majority of children being born at that time would never see The Milky Way with their own eyes. So make the effort to go to a dark sky place and take in the night sky.

Astrology is not part of this book and is a decision for the individual on how much credence they give it. However, we know from science, specifically astronomy, that we share this solar system with other planets, none of which, we believe, currently sustain life. However they move across the heavens and are wonders to behold with the naked eye, more so with binoculars or a telescope. One can see the rings around Saturn as a disc, or the moons of Jupiter as tiny dots of light adjacent to the planet, with binoculars and a steadying tripod on a clear night. From an astronomical perspective Jupiter is earth's protector, its gravity scooping up all the comets that would otherwise be bound for us. So maybe give a little thank you when you see it in the night sky.

The planets are part of the mythology of humanity, named after gods, inspiration for classical music, poetry and movies, even the name of a Disney character, although in 2006 Pluto was reclassified as a dwarf planet. Folklore has arisen around the planets, and astrology along with it, with each planet given a character, or a set of traits, perhaps reflecting back aspects of ourselves.

Even if their scientific influence is well known, the Sun, the Moon, the planets and the stars are natural wonders above us, to guide our way, provide light in the dark, to inspire dreams, fable and myth, and draw us to look deeper into the Universe, feeling connected to something bigger.

The Unimaginable

There is much that is difficult for us to comprehend and be aware of, especially if it is seemingly so detached from our day to day lives. From the minutely small to the extremely large, the invisible (to us) to the incomprehensibly big. But these things are worth thinking about, trying to comprehend, and perhaps re-framing or scaling to make more understandable.

Our Universe exploded into being about 13.8 billion years ago, Earth was formed some 4.5 billion years ago, the first microbial life about 3.5 billion years ago, complex life about 580 million years ago, and humanoids around 3 million years ago. A single calendar year can be used to represent this history of the Universe, a cosmic calendar, starting with the Big Bang at midnight Jan 1st, to now, just before midnight Dec 31st. The Earth would have coalesced around the beginning of September with the first life coming towards the end of that month. Complex life doesn't emerge until Dec 5th with humans arriving at about 22:24 Dec 31st. Homosapiens don't join the party until eight minutes to midnight Dec 31st and the past 500 years of human history are covered by just one second, from 23:59:59 to midnight Dec 31st!

However we are linked to all life across the history of our planet by the air we breathe, or more accurately to the 1% of our atmosphere that is the gas argon. Argon is an inert gas and does not combine readily with any other element, so has stayed airborne since the atmosphere first coalesced. This means the same argon atoms have been breathed by prehistoric animals, ancient peoples, and now us, and will be breathed by those to come after us. We are connected across the millennia by Argon, and similarly by the other inert gases, such as helium and neon. In fact, as matter is never destroyed only transformed, we are all made up of matter that has been recycled and re-purposed since it's creation during the big bang, and subsequently transmuted and redistributed by exploding super novae.

Our bodies are in a constant state of flux but are we aware of the self healing that is going on? The fighting off of infections and diseases, repairing broken bones or growing new cells? As previously mentioned (see *The North* section) our body's maintenance schedule replaces cells at varying rates, from a few days for the intestinal wall to seven to ten years for the whole skeleton. Then we have within our skull what has been referred to as the most complex structure in the known universe, our brain, which we still know very little about; not surprising with a conservatively estimated 500 trillion synapses firing away.

Then there is our sun, emitting a vast amount of energy, a fraction of which hits the Earth as electromagnetic waves. Out of these EM waves we, as humans, only see about $1/80^{th}$ of them as light and colour, the visible spectrum. The rest are invisible to our eyes and consist of gamma rays, x-rays and ultraviolet rays at the shorter wavelengths of light, infra red, microwaves and radio waves at the longer wavelengths. Are there other energies hidden from us? A spiritual energy, a frequency of consciousness, an energy of the divine?

The very, very large and the very, very small, are both difficult to imagine. But they can be made more understandable when scaled down or up. For example, lets take the population of world to be eight billion. If we take the cube root of eight billion the answer we get is two thousand. Eight billion could therefore be represented by a cube with dimensions 2000 x 2000 x 2000. If the cube was made up of grains of sand, each of which has a diameter of 0.5mm (about twenty thousandths of an inch), then this would give a cube of length 1m (just over 3 ft). A relatively small cube of sand representing the population of the planet, and hopefully not too difficult to imagine.

Now if we think about the number of atoms in the human body using the same grain of sand scale, then with approximately 7×10^{27} (a seven with twenty seven zeros after it) atoms in our bodies, we get a cube of sand with length just under 1000kms (around 600 miles - or the distance between London and Berlin). Slightly harder to imagine than a 1m cube but still feasible.... just.

(Cube root of 7×10^{27} = 1,913,000,000. With sand grains of 0.5mm diameter gives a cube side length of 956,500,000mm = 956.5kms or about 600miles)

Similarly in a 500ml (about 16fl oz) water bottle there are 17×10^{24} water molecules. So in one teaspoon (5ml) there are 17×10^{22} molecules of H_2O. The cube of sand to represent the molecules in a teaspoon of water would therefore be 27.5kms in length (17 miles). A seventeen mile high cube of sand to represent the number of molecules in one teaspoon of water. That's twice the height long haul passenger planes fly at!

(Cube root of 17×10^{22} = 55,000,000. With sand grains of 0.5mm diameter gives a cube side length of 27,500,000mm = 27.5kms or about 17 miles)

If we look at the very big such as our Solar System and beyond, then the figures are again mind boggling and of little meaning to us. The distance to our nearest neighbour the Moon is 384,000 kms (239,000 miles) whilst it is 150 million kms (93 million miles) to the Sun. Unfortunately, to fit on the pages of books and magazines, we have been brought up with disproportionate pictures of the solar system but more accurate representations are now available in videos on the internet. There are also scaled physical models of the solar system in Stockholm, Sweden, Zagreb, Croatia and Somerset, UK where the public can really get to grips with the sizes and distances of our part of the galaxy, especially with the walkable latter two installations.

The Somerset Space Walk, uses the tow path of the Bridgwater and Taunton canal to display proportional representations of the Sun and the eight planets, plus Pluto[21], along the 22km (14 mile) path using a scale of 1:530,000,000. The Sun is represented by a 2.5 metre (8.2 ft) wide fourteen ton concrete sphere located at Higher Maunsel lock, with the inner planets nearby, within 67 metres (220 ft), and Pluto, a tiny (just under 5mm (1/6th in)) diameter sphere on a plinth, an 11km (6.8 mile) walk away. On this scale the nearest star to our Solar System, Proxima Centauri, would be a red ball 37.5 centimetres (14.8 in) in diameter but impossible to site, as it would need to be 76,000 km (47,000 miles) away - roughly twice the circumference of the Earth!

Are we alone in the Universe?

It was such a cosmic coincidence that life began on earth that it is quite possible that we are alone in the Universe. There are likely to be bacteria or primitive organic matter on other worlds, if there is water present, but any form of complex and intelligent life may be

---

[21] As was constructed pre Pluto reclassification.

limited to our planet. The rare earth hypothesis states that Earth is the only place where life has begun due to the unique set of circumstances that have played out for life to begin here, such as our planet's distance from the Sun being within the *goldilocks* zone, the protection from asteroid impact provided by Jupiter, the atmosphere's ability to regulate temperature and reflect back into space dangerous cosmic rays, the magnetic field generated by the rotation of the iron core also deflecting harmful radiation, and the Moon keeping the Earth's tilt steady, with this tilt angle giving us the seasons and a stable enough environment for life to begin and ultimately thrive.

If we are alone that makes us a miracle, but of course we take life for granted. What other miracles are out there that may have passed many of us by? Are spirit encounters, spiritual or shamanic healings, or magical synchronicities, miracles that should be accepted? Instead of impossible they suddenly become possible.

Connecting with the unknown and unknowable

Contemplating the unknowable is akin to the Japanese koan, "what is the sound of one hand clapping?" The immediate answer seems impossible or out of reach. But by pondering the question, contemplating the unknowable, you are putting yourself in the space of someone who is open to learning. Being receptive to learning is the most important step in taking on-board new knowledge. As any teacher knows, the student ready and willing to learn will be a joy to have in the class. The student that is not receptive (for whatever reason) will not be engaged, be easily distracted, become bored and even disruptive, affecting all others in the class.

How does one put oneself in a state of openness and to contemplate the unknowable? The most obvious way is by meditating. Meditation is a good place to take steps towards connecting to whatever is inside and outside of oneself. To link to that which is known and to that which is unknown, or even unknowable, by clearing the mind and just being, and just allowing.

So when in meditation allow yourself to connect with the Universe, to go out into the cosmos or up to heaven. Meet Great Spirit, God, Goddess or that which is beyond, whatever you call *it*. If *it* is beyond your understanding or comprehension, or outside of your comfort zone, then purely accept this as being so, but also accept that maybe *it* can hear you or *it* can be with you. You don't have to call *it* God, or spirit, or anything that you are not comfortable with, but you have to call *it* something. I suggest try just calling *it* the Universe and go from there. As you are part of this universe then maybe also accept that *it* maybe part of you too, and not separate from you.

Another method of connecting with the unseen is to observe the effects of the known invisible (to humans) forces. Throwing a ball in the air and seeing it come back down again shows us the effect of gravity, the warmth of the Sun is evidence of the infra-red rays emitted, whilst sunburn is the result of overexposure to the Sun's strong ultraviolet rays. Fridge magnets and a directional compass (hopefully you have one in your tool kit) clearly show the effects of magnetism. All unseen but measurable with the right scientific equipment. But are there unseen forces and energies that still remain hidden to science?

Heaven and Earth flow

This is similar to some of the previous breath flow exercises but with a more physical approach, using movement to create a flow of energy from above and below. Begin by standing tall and grounding yourself, imagining roots coming from your feet going deep into the earth. Squat down and bring your arms down in front of you, sweeping your hands across your legs, in a gathering earth energy motion and then slowly stand, pulling this energy up with your hands, through your feet and into your body. As you reach your chest turn your hands so you can continue the motion, but now pushing the energy through the upper body, into the head and out of your crown and fingertips, as your arms sweep up and extend above you to the heavens. Reverse the movement, pulling energy from the Universe down through the top of your head, through your body, turning your hands over halfway and then pushing it through the lower body, out of your feet and down into the earth.

Imagine brown earthy energy, red molten lava or water being pulled up from the earth and flowing through your body, before being pushed out of the top of your head and outstretched arms towards the sky. Whatever colour feels right to you is fine. Conversely visualise sunlight (gold), moonlight (silver), a mix of both (platinum), or maybe a white or indigo spiritual light, when pulling energy down from above, and letting it flow through your body and into the ground. Breathe in when pulling in, from above or below, and breathe out when pushing out, up or down. Keep the movements flowing and find a rhythm.

Vary the visualisation and note any different effects. Swap between pulling up red magma, green grass or blue ocean water, and pulling down twinkling starlight, a colourful rainbow or a divine violet.

Connect with what is above

Feel the connections in nature that are above or that move in an upwards direction. Trees growing, reaching for the light; an eagle soaring and swooping; flames, sparks and smoke darting up from a fire and drifting away into the sky. Lose yourself in cloud formations. Dream upon the vapour trails of planes as they pass overhead, wondering what far flung places they are headed to. Watch sunrises and sunsets and be in awe. Notice how the wildlife around you, the birds for example behave at this time of the day. Lay on the ground under a stand of trees and gaze up along their trunks skyward. Climb up high, on a hill or mountain and take in the view.

Always take in the view.

Communication

The use of language to communicate (the English language in the case of this book) is necessary but has its limitations and can be open to misinterpretation. As we probably all know (and have been guilty of), any form of texting, social media posting or emailing can easily be misunderstood or *taken the wrong way* by the reader. Shortened sentences, bullet points or headlines do not convey the full meaning intended. Additionally some words are far more loaded, and can be open to various interpretations depending on a person's beliefs or viewpoint. Words such as love, god, goddess, spiritual, religion, power and energy for example, may well have dictionary definitions but their use in conveying a certain meaning vary greatly. Then there are cultural and translational differences, namely between the languages of countries, regions and provinces, even between towns in the same area. The same words can have various meanings, or mean slightly different things, especially when translated from one language to another. There is also the issue of comprehension and the use of vocabulary that may not be fully understood by the recipient. The written and spoken word alone are not enough for true communication.

Communication begins at an early age, even from before birth, whilst in the womb. Talking to baby, playing music and creating a good atmosphere can all have an effect upon the unborn child. The emotional and psychological state of the mother also has a profound effect upon the developing baby. In the Channel 4 TV programme *Grayson Perry: Rites of Passage*, Dr Cyriac, consultant paediatrician at Broomfield hospital, Essex, UK, noted:

> *"If a mother is distraught... if I can reassure her and she leaves with a smiley face I know the child will be ok, as it is the vibrations of the mother which is actually the healing for the child... Happy mother equals a happy child."*

The child feels and takes on emotions and energy from it's mother, as I am sure any mother would attest to. From the father too, be it his voice, emotional tone or maybe just his energy when nearby. Maybe also from any other person that is regularly in close contact with the mother during the pregnancy. This communication is clearly not understood verbally by the unborn infant, rather it is received as non verbal, chemical and energetic in nature. The non verbal component of communication is vital to comprehension, as can be illustrated if we have ever tried to make ourselves understood in a foreign country where we do not speak the local language, using tone, expressions and gesticulation only. This non verbal component is also at work when we talk to people or watch interviews, where the words spoken do not seem to match the behaviour or bodily cues of the speaker, sometimes leaving us feeling unconvinced by what they have said, maybe even giving us the impression that they do not believe what they are saying, are acting, or are just plain lying. Non verbal communication experts can be very valuable in interview scenarios or as political correspondents to the media.

Take this a step further and one will see that underlying this non verbal communication is the intention of the communicator to impart a meaning, both sub-consciously when being genuine, or consciously when trying to persuade or mislead. The thought form that drives this intention can be deemed as the energy of the intention. In our conscious lives we are constantly thinking and therefore creating these thought forms, normally in our native language. If it is questionable how much is communicated through language, through words alone, then we must be cautious when listening to our own internal monologue. Perhaps we should be more focused on the imagery our minds create as an accompaniment to our the words.

If we close our eyes (or just soften our focus), we can visualise, imagine and create pictures internally. We know that a picture paints a thousand words and it is no different in our minds. The image we conjure up can capture and impart much more meaning than a string of sentences. But what we are actually trying to do is capture the emotion or feeling of a situation or an idea. This is, in part, the goal of an artist. They produce their work to impart emotions and sensations, not just create a beautiful image or object. The artist wants to stir up feelings and delve into emotions that are, by nature difficult to describe, but far easier to feel.

Visualisations and self help exercises (including many of those detailed in this book) are used to recreate scenarios and situations where we can manifest or tap into particular emotions and feelings, and embody them to some degree. This can lead us to expressing and releasing any harmful emotions in a safe and conscious way, rather than letting them overwhelm or hijack us in our daily lives, or feel we are a slave to them, or the negative feelings they can carry. Moreover, visualisations of successful scenarios allow us to feel and live through desired outcomes, creating the neurological pathways in our brain and a field of desired intentional energy within our body, familiarising us with this vibration of achievement. This ability to imagine ourselves winning is a powerful tool, used by many professionals from athletes to entrepreneurs, politicians to military leaders, and can be adapted to any life situation where we feel we need a self administered boost.

Unwanted emotions and feelings, repeating negative monologues or thought forms, can also be sidelined by going into silence through meditation, taking us beyond the chattering mind and diminishing their impact somewhat, allowing us to take back control. Meditation, can take many forms, from the closed eyes, sitting quietly type, to the active meditations of walking, cleaning, playing an instrument, chanting, driving, or listening to music. Any activity where we feel engaged totally, on auto pilot, or in the flow, is a form of meditation. We are trying to move away from our ego selves and open up to the flow of life and, in a sense, commune with something outside of ourselves.

Communication with people is one thing but what about with the more-than-human world, with animals, plants or even the elements of earth, wind, fire, water and air? All pet owners know that their animal understands them to some degree, albeit not a comprehension of the spoken words, but a mixture of the tone, gesture or positive reinforcement (through treats or affection) when a desired behaviour is displayed. If we encounter a wild animal we are not looking to control its behaviour but I am sure we would all like to communicate with it.

Dr Doolittle aside, how would we talk to the animals? Well, exactly as we would talk to anyone else. The words we say are not understood by the animal, but if we are genuine the thought form, the non verbal communication and the energy of our intention can be imparted. Pets and animals in captivity pick up on this. Owners of horses know how responsive to emotion a horse can be, hence their use in mental health therapy, especially with children, who are naturally emotionally sensitive and have not built up the internal ego blocks of adults. Being with animals, especially pets that we can touch and hold, offer many benefits to our state of well being, from the tactile contact of another living creature to the emotional boost of the animal's companionship and the often unconditional love given.

After a period of training, pets or working animals may associate the sound of a word we say with a particular command, but they do not comprehend the word being said. They have their own language. As do all animals and, for that matter, all organisms. Michael Prime, a guest on the BBC TV programme *Autumnwatch*, has developed an instrument to measure the feint bio-electrical signals produced by fungi that fluctuate depending on the state of the fungus. His equipment then converts these fungal communications into audible electronic noises. Michael has also recorded other plant life, and has used these sounds in art installations, audio tracks and even recorded a number of cds.

Trees too have their methods of communication, one of which (as previously mentioned) is by connecting with other trees via their roots and the underground network of fungal mycelium strands. Using this *wood-wide-web* network a tree can send help messages for required nutrients that other trees in the area may be able to provide, or signal a warning to local trees of an attack from a pest, an unwanted bacterium or fungus, giving the other trees time to raise their defences. The language of the trees of course is not English, but rather chemical and electrical signals. However, underlying communication is the desire to impart a meaning, in this case, 'I need nutrients', or 'warning, harmful beetle infestation.' The tree is communicating with an energy of intention, which could be argued as showing a form of intelligence.

So if a tree can communicate can we as humans commune with it? If we touch, hug or sit under a tree, and allow space for the tree's form of communication to merge with ours, that is, to allow their energy of intention to manifest within us in the form of imagery, emotions and feelings, then I believe such communication is possible. The tree has a basic level of understanding of our intention, generated through our thought form and imparted energy, rather than comprehending any words spoken. In fact I suggest this is the case for all plant and animal life, and to some degree with the elements and inanimate objects. Botanists, horticulturists and many gardeners are well versed with talking to their plants, whilst zoo keepers, horse whisperers and pet reiki practitioners all commune with the animals they care for. There is also a communication going on when we sit around a fire, swim in a river, stand on a cliff in the wind or put our hands in the earth as we tend the soil. This may be seemingly one way, and purely on an emotional level, but only the barrier of a rigid indoctrinated belief that this is impossible stops us from attempting to make it two way. However we can communicate with the more-than-human world, at some level, via intention, connection and energy, but to do so we must make the effort to tune in, open up all of our senses and create space for the communication to take place.

This has been a cornerstone of shamanic practice throughout history as from a shamanic viewpoint, everything is alive, has it's own spirit and energy, and is linked by the web of life. From the trees and plants to the rocks and mountains, from the raindrops to the oceans, from the wind to the stars, it is all in a harmonious conversation of being. We can join in that communication, simply by conversing with nature, by talking, sensing, or feeling, and allowing our intention to come from the heart. If we are still, open and patient then the conversation may be two way, with a response coming in the form of a feeling, an image in our mind, or even a real time sign from nature, in the form of a sound, an object stumbled upon, or an animal encounter.

As humans we are drawn to natural objects and will often touch them, like to hold them or just enjoy looking at them. Wooden objects, rocks and crystals, shells, plants and flowers, all have special places in our homes. If there is a natural object that you like to hold, or feel connected to in some way, then maybe it is trying to communicate with you. There is an energetic vibration emanating from the object which you are drawn to, or resonate with, a message for you being spoken without words. Try sitting in meditation or journeying whilst holding the object. Often these objects can be seen as talismen, that over time may seem to take on magical properties, especially if they have been used effectively in healing work, on ourselves or with others. More accepted as having potent properties are the chemically active compounds found in nature, used in their raw form by herbalists, healers and lay folk with a little knowledge, and synthesised by chemists into modern medicines.

So with talismen, objects from nature and natural remedies in mind, clearly there is some truth in the stories of the medicine cabinets of witches and wizards being full of interesting natural objects.
(Please note though, I am totally against the hunting, farming or exploitation of animals for their body parts, as often associated with traditional Chinese medicine.)

Our body also communicates. Our physiological systems are connected and communicate via the nervous and endocrine systems, feeding back information on internal health, in the form of pains, palpitations, or sensations for example, through the hormonal generation of certain feelings and emotions, and by informing us of our external world, via our senses. This direct communication is coupled with more sublime forms such as our intuition, the vibrations we pick up upon from other people or places, and our night-time dreams and the metaphors within; all ways in which something outside of our immediate consciousness in trying to get our attention.

Nature expresses herself, for want of a better word, naturally. We, as humans, have evolved a language of words to try and express ourselves, but often fall short when it comes to conveying the totality of what we truly want to say. We are limited by language and our own vocabulary. Writers, poets and playwrights have strived to rectify this when they attempt to describe the human condition, as do other artists, be it with an evocative painting, ethereal drawing or sublime sculpture, the chef that stirs something deep inside with the presentation, smell and taste of their exquisite food, or the musician tugging at our heartstrings.

Perhaps the best form of musical expression is classical music, without lyrics to misinterpret, allowing the listener to be taken away solely on the sounds of the instruments and the emotions evoked by the composition. At a more basic level, sound repetition such as chanting, mantra reciting, drum beating or rattle shaking can occupy the ego mind and create the space for communication to take place with something outside of ourselves. We just have to be open to it.

The Centre - Sovereignty, balance, and authenticity

*"We are all masters of our own destiny. We can so easily
make the same mistakes over and over. We can so easily
flee from everything that we desire and which life so
generously places before us.
Alternatively, we can surrender ourselves to Divine
Providence, take God's hand, and fight for our dreams,
believing that they always arrive at the right moment."*
Paul Cohelo, Brida.

Ultimately, life is up to you. Whatever your background, whatever experiences you have had, whatever setbacks and traumas have befallen you, the colour of your skin, gender or nationality, your life is your responsibility, nobody else's. It is up to you what you make of it. Being dictated to by another (be it a person, company, government or culture), following blindly and letting life happen to you, or blaming circumstances, environment, parents, society, religion, God or any other deity about the state of your life, will not help in the long run. Do you have a relationship to life, to the more-than-human world that is outside of *you,* spiritual or otherwise? Are you in control of this, or is it something that is inherited or you feel obliged to conform to?

Working on yourself will highlight areas that may need improving, or where the negative influences can be lessened, showing where you can change your thoughts, behaviours and habits. You can find deeper meaning, more value in all things, see beyond the day to day and accept differences, both in yourself and in others.

To sit at the centre of all that is inside and outside of you, requires the ability to be a witness; to recognise, to understand and to take appropriate action; to adapt, change, incorporate, accept, or let go of; to be courageous; to ask for help, and to listen for and act upon the answer; to show compassion; and to be confident in yourself, even if you do not have all the answers. But in doing all this you realise that you are at the centre. You are in charge. You have to take responsibility. This is sovereignty. King or queen (or both) of all you have influence over.

The law of attraction

If one has read spiritual books, gone to workshops or listened to spiritual advice, then the law of attraction is always to be found. I'm not sure who made it law and I have no doubt it can be broken, however, the general premise behind it is sound, if only now science, and in particular, the science of quantum, is beginning to understand why. It comes from the idea that our thoughts create our reality. The energy behind our thoughts, that speed of light impulse, is creative in its intention. This links into consciousness and the vast resource of creative energy held therein, currently beyond scientific measure but one day surely to be observed and clarified.

As this law is indiscriminate negative and positive thoughts are treated as the same. Therefore you need to make a conscious effort to drop negative thinking and stay focussed on the positives. Focus on what you DO want, not on what you don't want. Continually worrying about what you don't want to happen only draws it closer to you.

Notice when negative thoughts come up. Catch them, block them or re-frame them into a positive. In *The Power Within You Now!* Sue Stone says:

> *"When a thought (vibration) is repeated the brain attaches emotion to it, this is stored in the subconscious and acted upon behind the scenes. Good or bad, positive or negative, true or false, the subconscious does not differentiate. Where conscious thoughts are leading, the subconscious will follow."*

So start by putting yourself in an open and receptive state, ideally in a state of love. Visualise love in any way you wish - a partner, a child, a love of life, a love of nature, a love of yourself. Breathe deeply into the heart and let the expression of love expand throughout your body, and travel outwards as far and wide and as all embracing as you wish. Next move your focus on to what you wish to attract and draw into your life. Visualise yourself already having it. Bring it alive in your heart, allowing the experience to flow through you. Feel it flow to other parts of your body. Finally remember or call up the feeling of gratitude in appreciation of what you wish to receive, knowing that it is coming to you. Again starting in the heart area and allowing it to spread throughout your body, spending time in this place of gratitude.

Visualise and embody the life you want as though it is already here. Working with affirmations, visualisations and your vision board can help with this. However, please note that positive thinking alone, without embracing the feelings of being successful or achieving your desires, is likely to fail and leave you disappointed and disillusioned. As will be mentioned later the ancient philosophers of the stoic and similar schools realised that the highs (and lows) of life should be seen as outside judgements (and to some degree psychological imposters), and a form of detachment should be cultivated, to help lead a calmer and more peaceful, even happier life.

Archetypes and characteristics

We all have certain characteristics. Some inherited, others developed over our lives. Psychologists have given labels to these generalised characteristics and use them to differentiate and distinguish people, perhaps showing where strengths or weaknesses lie. Such categorising includes the Warrior, Settler or Nomad, as described by hypnotherapist Terrence Watts[22] to profile our subconscious drivers, the sixteen personality types as outlined in the Myers-Briggs test used by recruitment consultants to streamline job candidates, and the roles people play in teams, such as those described by Belbin, to help corporations develop the optimal team structures. All are based around the personality and characteristics of the individual and how they interact with others and the world.

As an experiment during my studies at university I devised a questionnaire, completed by my fellow classmates, that would broadly show which of the Belbin team roles they would fall into. These nine roles Belbin proposed are Resource Investigator, Teamworker and Co-ordinator (the Social roles); Plant, Monitor Evaluator and Specialist (the Thinking roles), and Shaper, Implementer and Completer Finisher (the Action or Task roles). I then split the class into a number of smaller groups, based on these characteristics, to carry out a simple team work exercise. I purposely comprised each team with people that had the same or similar characteristics, e.g., a group comprised of only the social roles, or another of thinking roles only. There was one team, however, that I

---

[22] Terrence Watts, *Warriors, Settlers and Nomads*, 2000, Crown House Publishing.

formed with one of each of the Belbin team roles, that outperformed the others and completed the task first, and with the least amount of team friction. This clearly demonstrated how people or groups of people can be chosen, worked with or manipulated based upon their character. It also highlights were certain traits may be lacking or the areas for the individual to work upon if they wish to grow. Perhaps a more soulful and nature connected viewpoint on archetypes is that as described by Bill Plotkin in his book *Wild Mind* and termed the *four facets of wholeness*[23]:

- *Nurturing Generative Adult*: Compassionate, courageous, competent, knowledgeable, and exhibits heart-centred thinking; i.e., independent, critical, creative, moral. A benevolent king or queen, spiritual or peaceful warrior, mature and caring mother and father.

- *Innocent/Sage*: Able to see the bigger picture, innocent, wise, clear-minded, light-hearted, wily, extroverted, and exhibits full-presence sensing; i.e., alive to the five senses. Represented by the sacred fool or trickster, priest, priestess, guide to spirit.

- *Wild indigenous one*: Emotive, sensuous, instinctive, playful, erotic-sexual, fully at home in the human body and in the more-than-human world and exhibits full-body feeling; i.e., gut feeling, body and organ awareness, hunches, vibes, sexual passion, in touch with emotions. Represented by Pan, Artemis/Diana, the Green Man.

- *Muse/Inner beloved*: Imaginative, erotic-romantic, idealistic, visionary, adventurous, darkness savouring, introverted, and exhibits deep imagination; i.e., images, dreams and visions. Represented by magician, wanderer, hermit, psychopomp, anima/animas, guide to soul.

---

[23] Bill Plotkin, *Wild Mind: A Field Guide to the Human Psyche*, 2013, New World Library.

These archetypes are at play when we are pulled by a calling to discover more about life and our part to play within it. Bill calls this *the descent to the Soul*[24] (a western and contemporary take on adult initiation) and is similar to the journey Carl Jung took that eventually led to the field of depth psychology.

Acceptance

We are all different, but we are all connected. Therefore at the root of balance, harmony, integration, diversity, community and society, is acceptance. Acceptance of race, religion, culture, sexual orientation, politics, education, character, and the right to an opinion. These also are the obvious areas of difference. And most notably when we see or hear something we are not familiar with, don't like or disagree with.

Differences crop up in less obvious ways too. Take smell for example, probably the most evocative of the senses. This is often forgotten when it comes to acceptance. Like it or not, we all have our own odour, the way we smell to others, with many of us using fragrances, in the form of perfume, aftershave or deodorant, to change or mask our aroma. There are also pheromones at play here, our natural scent. This helps when meeting a potential partner. Liking their smell is a positive and often arousing sign. Not liking their smell is a good indicator that maybe you are not compatible as mates or life long partners.

Similarly with sound. Again, as we all have our own aroma, we all have our own sound; our accent, our dialect, the way in which we speak, and obviously the language of our region or country. It forms part of our cultural identity. Inherited and learnt. We accept other

---

[24] Bill Plotkin, *The Journey of Soul Initiation: A Field Guide for Visionaries, Revolutionaries, and Evolutionaries,* 2021, New World LIbrary.

people's accents (even if we may not like them) but we don't dismiss them as people because of how they speak. The vocal taunts or accent mimicry between rival countries, for example, Australia, England and USA, is accepted as being sarcasm and banter between citizens (predominately male, it must be said), and often around sporting competitions. In the current climate though this is often viewed as veiled racism. I find this hard to accept. It is, in my experience, part of the gamesmanship between competitive egos rather than in any way racist.

Additionally it is not racist not to like a particular accent, or how someone sounds. As with smell, it is just human nature. Not liking how someone sounds is the same as not liking their aroma, how they dress or anything else about them. It is just a natural, almost primal, reaction to the unfamiliar, and not racist. Imagine a pupil starting mid term at a new school. This pupil comes from another part of the country and has a strong regional accent. There is a chance he will be made fun of for his accent by some of the other students, being taunted or having his words repeated back to him in an exaggerated comical way. On the other hand some may find his voice attractive, not only due to the sound of his accent, but also because it separates him from the rest, makes him stand out from the crowd.

As creatures of habit we are comfortable with the familiar; our routines, the people we work and share our life with, our community. Change or the unfamiliar; new places, new people, new ideas, can be a challenge and initially difficult to accept. Often though, with time, we become familiar with the new and can accept the differences, even come to embrace them.

Moving to a new home, in a new area, with new neighbours, takes time to *settle* into. If this is to a different country then this may be more challenging than if it's to another street in the same town.

A simpler example of acceptance over time is that of trying a new hot drink, or removing sugar from tea or coffee. Initially you may not like it, it may even disgust you, but over time your taste buds adjust, and you accept the new drink, even come to enjoy it.

Then there is the more obvious area of how someone looks. For example, their facial features, body shape and size, the colour of their skin, their clothing, their mannerisms and how they carry themselves. Again we are attracted to certain traits and characteristics, indifferent or not attracted to others, and in the mating game often we are more attracted to those that look similar to ourselves, we are familiar with, or conform to the archetype we are normally attracted to (giving us the phrase, "he/she is not my type".) Of course this is not always the case and beauty is never only skin deep.

Taking this one step further, we also have our own energy. You may link this to character and thereby say our character dictates the energy we put out into the world. Some people captivate a room when they walk into it, others seemingly can suck the atmosphere out. These are extremes and clearly the vast majority lie somewhere in the middle. In the hump of the statistical bell shaped *normal* curve.

So it is clearly easy to accept and understand that we as individuals don't like the same things, prefer certain smells over others, have a particular palette when it comes to taste and what pleases the ear. The same can be said of physical appearance, skin colour, size, or any other physical attribute. Again this is not being racist, this is just natural. Racism, along with other -isms (i.e., sex, size, age), is excluding or chastising, penalising and bringing attention to differences for reasons of coercion, exploitation, abuse or entertainment. There is a distinction. We are all different, we all have different tastes and preferences, but we can treat everyone with respect, accepting each other, differences and all. The mind is powerful and can overcome the senses and our instinctual resistance with some effort, allowing us to see beyond the animalistic impulses of our mammalian brain, and feel love for any and all people, and any and all animals for that matter. Where in your life do you struggle with acceptance of differences, and of others? Where perhaps are you being quick to judge?

The Doorway

Be standing to do this exercise, with enough space to take a step forward, turn around, and step back. Close your eyes or wear a blindfold to go into darkness. Begin by imagining an ornate door set into a beautiful doorway in front of you, with a key on a hook off to one side. Take the key and unlock the door. Turn the handle and open the door away from you, unveiling a beautiful world beyond. Take a step through the doorway into this imaginary domain, both in your mind and also physically in the place you are standing in the ordinary world. As you cross the threshold sense that you are leaving behind all of your troubles and issues in the ordinary world, even if only briefly, and are stepping into a magical world of possibility, of new opportunity and a place of miracles. Actively feel the old life being left behind you, as something you have stepped away from. Feel your problems, worries or concerns all dissipate. They mean nothing in this brave new world you have stepped into.

Explore the landscape through this doorway. What does it look and feel like? Who or what exists here? Converse with this world. Call out, ask for help. Question things and beings. Is there a stone circle here? If not why not create one? Step into it and continue the conversation and your journey in this realm. This is a world of creation. What does your heart and your soul want to create in this world? What dreams do you want to explore? Take time to explore this magical place and become familiar with it.

When you feel you have finished, return to the doorway and face it looking back at your old life. It is there waiting for you if you want it, just as you left it a moment ago. However to the right is another doorway, also leading back to the ordinary world, but this time it is a new life, a new start, without the attachments of the previous life. Make your choice and walk through. Again as you take the step across the threshold in your visualisation, also physically do so in the ordinary world. The door will automatically gently close behind you, but know that this is a place you are welcome to return to, and explore whenever you wish, and perhaps from a new perspective.

Bring yourself back into the ordinary world, removing any blindfold and opening your eyes.

Lighthouse keeper exercise

This exercise is to put you at the centre of the storm, at the heart of the tempest, but able to weather it, knowing you are being looked after. Visualise yourself as a lighthouse keeper, on a rocky outcrop in the ocean, open to the elements, but protected. Your light keeps shining, lighting the way and warning of rocks and danger. Allow a storm to rage around you as you watch it from the safety of your lighthouse, almost in the elements but safe from harm. Feel the power but not the fear. Feel the sturdiness of the structure you are standing in, it's capability to withstand the forces of nature thrown at it, rooted to the rock. Unmoving, unbending, unyielding. Feel these traits within yourself. Feel strong, powerful, resilient and grounded, whatever is going in your life or the world around you.

Note: Safety Warning. This exercise can be enhanced if carried out during a storm, either in your home, or sheltering safely somewhere outside, being mindful of any strong winds, falling branches or lightning.

Anchors and power places

What are your anchors? Those things that talk directly to your soul, enrich you beyond words and can bring you back to feeling connected, to feeling yourself, or maybe even provide an inkling towards your purpose and place in this world? What do you turn to in a time of need or when you want to be uplifted and re-energised? And to what places do you go? Where do you feel at home, at peace, connected, inspired, feel yourself or comfortable being lost in the moment? Some examples of anchors are making, lighting and gazing at a real fire; the smell of smoke from a wood fire; holding a treasured talisman; spending time in nature; painting; working with wood; beating a drum; playing music; meditating; baking; the smell of the forest; exercise; sea air; a hot water bottle on your belly; knitting; chanting or singing; taking photographs; holding objects from your altar; being with your partner. Anything can be an anchor for you, maybe having its root in your childhood, like a love of fishing, stroking a pet, or standing out in the rain under an umbrella.

Similarly power places can be anywhere; the beach; a certain bench in the park; your garden; under a tree; on a cliff top; at your football team's ground; a particular cafe or museum; standing in the wind or rain; your bedroom; on top of a mountain. You may have many, and be drawn to each for a different reason.

Do you have a sit spot? A place in nature that you are drawn to and can come back to throughout the year to notice the changing of the seasons. It is a place where you can sit quietly and connect with the nature around you, become familiar with any plants, trees, or animals and the geology and geography of the area. Conversely, the more time you spend here, the more the flora and fauna of the area become familiar with you and your own energy. Try conversing with nature when in your sit spot, asking your deepest questions.

List out your anchors and power places, noticing any crossover or themes. What have remained since you were young? What ones are new? Are there others you are drawn to but never explored?

Route home

This is a simple yet often illuminating exercise. Write down the people connections that have led you to where you are today. By that I mean who have you met through someone else, or by introduction from another, that have brought you to where you are now? Include relatives, friends, teachers, colleagues, or anyone else who was a key link in your life chain. Start from now and take the linkage back to your parents and where you were born.

For example, let's say you met your romantic partner at your company's annual conference; you joined the company due to an introduction from an ex-colleague; you met your ex-colleague on a meditation course; you went on this course on a friend's recommendation; you knew your friend since school; you went to the school you did because your parents decided to live in that area. Would you have met your partner if there was a break in this chain? Take a moment to give thanks to each one of the people in your route home.

Balance

As human beings we believe we can handle the pace of change we see on our planet, as we can make use of our brains to be flexible and adapt. Nature takes longer. The natural world's *brain* runs to a slower beat. It has taken many years for the balance to be struck between all living organisms in an ecosystem. Recovery from changes to that system takes time. But restoring the balance is inevitable. Nature is programmed that way. To find balance.

This is true for humanity too. Deep down our natural instinct is to find balance. However our minds and egos have taken over somewhat and we are often pulled away from balance by outside influences. Influences from our culture, our upbringing and the media all pull at us, demanding that we behave in a particular way, conform to specific ideals or philosophies, are coerced into buying particular things, or look a certain way to fit in. This constant bombardment, and strain on our psyches, does not lend itself to balance.

So we have to take responsibility and move ourselves out of this daily drama of life and find our own way of being and our own balance. Meditation and other spiritual pursuits lend themselves to this, even if only practised for a few minutes a day. Just touching base with our internal selves, taking time to recognise where we may be out of balance, and taking steps to rectify this, is often enough to keep us content. The routine chores, daily struggles, and unexpected issues that arise will always be there, especially in a western society, as will fears around safety, health, relationships and financial security. Allowing ourselves a brief moment of calm will act as an oasis of balance, in what can be a fraught daily life.

Globally, being in balance has always been recognised as being worthwhile. In the three thousand year old indian holistic healing system of Ayurveda, balancing your doshas (the three bio-energy centres of vata, pitta and kapha) is important to physical and digestive health. Yoga too incorporates finding your own balance physically, whilst being in, and moving into and out of, certain postures called asanas. This married with yogic breathing techniques (known as pranayama; meaning 'controlling life energy with the breath' in sanskrit) can help calm nerves, find balance, be useful in meditation, transmute negativity, and help heal the body.

Tai-chi, qi-gong or practices based around flowing movements, again requiring physical balance, can lead to a mental calmness. The Chinese philosophy of yin and yang also shows how balance is needed, often between two conflicting parts of the psyche, to create the whole. This has been taken onboard by psychologists too, where a balance between the mental archetypes is often sought, to make an individual whole from a psychological perspective.

Being in balance is not about being in the middle or normal, it is knowing when you are being too much of one thing and not enough of it's opposite. For example, when cultivating a balance with nature you don't have to up sticks and to go and live sustainably in the forest. Maybe just spending more time walking in a natural setting, away from urban life and its trappings, will be beneficial.

Emotional Freedom Technique (EFT)

Tapping on the body has been mentioned a number of times in this book and worthy of further investigation if you have found it useful. According to EFT proponents, tapping on certain areas, most commonly acupuncture points, has a calming and therapeutic effect, helping with disorders, imbalances and such ailments as headaches, pains or anxiety. I have found tapping extremely helpful when it comes to clearing blocks and triggering an emotional release when used within a practice or ceremony, normally around letting go. Particular points to tap are the throat, the left upper chest, belly area or karate chop point on the hands.

Talismen

Talismen are objects that are sacred or special to you. Ones that you regularly keep with you, in a pocket, on a key chain, or worn as jewellery. They could be objects from nature, a conker, a stone, a shell, a crystal, a piece of wood, or man made items such as a badge, ring, necklace, small toy or ornament. Ideally keep them on your altar when they are not with you, and decide after any daily meditation, affirmation or prayers, which one you wish to work with through the day. These are reminders of your connection to that which is outside of your conscious self. I suggest only carrying or wearing one or two items each day, thus focusing the energy. Lucky objects are only lucky because of the creative energy that is associated with them.

Beautiful objects are inherently powerful because of their innate beauty to us. They do not have to be expensive. An acorn in it's cup, a pressed flower, a small trinket, all can have profound meaning. For many years I have used conkers, as I like how they feel in my hand and the direct connection with nature they provide. One can be found in most of my coat and jacket pockets, allowing me to easily tap into this connection to something bigger as I hold it, even if whilst on a train or walking the city streets.

The phrase "touch wood", uttered after a statement of purpose and hoping for some good fortune, accompanied by feeling something wooden (comically often your head if there is no wood nearby), has only come in to modern parlance because of the importance of trees and wood throughout our history, and the powerful and almost magical properties wood exhibits. So why shouldn't touching it or being near it, impart some of that magic? That is how we humans often think. Being next to something (or someone) powerful, or deemed lucky, enhances us by association and proximity. This leads nicely on to the idea of energetic fields and the auras that all life emanate.

Energetic fields and auras

We are constantly surrounded by fields of energy in our daily lives. There is a long list of detectable particles bombarding us all day every day, many of which we are blissfully unaware of. From the cosmic microwave background radiation generated at the dawn of time during the Big Bang, to the movement of the Earth's molten iron core creating a global magnetic field. But perhaps most significant is the radiation from our star. The Sun emits all wavelengths of the electromagnetic spectrum, from the visible to the invisible. Infra-red, ultraviolet, microwave, x-rays, gamma rays, etc., all of which travel for eight minutes across the vacuum of space to arrive here on Earth and interact with the atmosphere, the land and seas, and are fundamental in the survival of nearly all life on this planet in one way or another.

The human body emits its own energies too, in the form of heat, sound, electrical pulses and magnetic fields, generated by our heart and nervous system. We also emit and detect chemical signals or pheromones, just as many other animal species do, often to attract a mate. Animals also use energy signatures as part of their daily lives, as a tool for food foraging, territory marking, nest locating, or for navigating migratory routes.

The planet is awash with signals, both naturally occurring and, ever more so nowadays, man made. It is not a surprise then that some people find themselves overloaded with sensory input, and may even feel physically unwell by the signals that surround and pass through them on a daily basis. Some have had to resort to living off grid, or perhaps more correctly, a distance away from the grid, to be able to live healthily. Power grids and telecommunications masts are definitely a problem for some of the acutely sensitive in our society.

We know about being attracted to, indifferent about or repulsed by certain people, based often on how they present themselves, their physical appearance, their pheromones or odour, their tone and accent, and their mannerisms and behaviour. These qualities, picked up upon through our senses, all feed into our impression of them. But what about any other form of energy that people emit? Is there a spiritual energy? Some sensitive people may well be able to tune into this energy, even to the energies of those that are deceased (i.e., psychics), just as others can tune in to the natural world (i.e., gardeners), to animals (i.e., vets), to their bodies (i.e., yogis) and to other people (i.e., psychologists).

According to mainstream science, seeing or measuring human spiritual energy is currently not possible. However, there are those people sensitive enough (or psychic enough) who say they are able to see the energy a person emits, or their aura, and often linking the colours they sense with certain spiritual insight. There is a form of photography that has gained some popularity amongst spiritual circles as being able to capture the aura around a person. It is based on the work of Russian scientist Semyon Kirlian, and developed into an aura camera by Guy Coggins in California in the 1980s. The photographs may be colourful but there is no evidence as to their credibility.

However there is something at play here as the majority of people, whether they call themselves spiritual or not, can pick up on the energies of places and the emotions of others. For example, have you ever felt uneasy stepping into a certain bar, restaurant or shop due to the architecture, the *atmosphere*, or maybe one or more of the people inside? Are you drawn to (or repelled by) certain places for no apparent reason? Have you ever been attracted to a particular person at a gathering, can feel their *good vibes*, or conversely, almost become physically sick by being too near certain people for an extended period of time? Many spiritual people find it difficult to be in crowds or travel on congested public transport, especially in confined spaces such as the London Underground, as they pick up on the abundance of energy (normally deemed chaotic or negative) with no way to escape it.

If you find you are highly sensitive, or maybe feeling out of sorts for no apparent reason, maybe you are picking up on some form of negative (or negatively perceived) energy from a person you spend time with, or from your local area, a place you frequent, or even from the media. Spending too much time watching and reading the mainstream news or swiping through social media, can have a major effect on your energy levels. A constant stream of depressing and worrying reports can take its toll on the human psyche. Over prolonged periods this can have an influence on the physical, often being noticed firstly in the gut. Of course, spending too much time looking at electronic devices, whatever the reason, is also unhealthy.

As previously mentioned, living near power lines has an effect on some people, as can living near other man made objects, especially those not in-keeping with the natural landscape, such as grey, angular, concrete high rise apartment blocks, noisy congested roads or motorways, busy airports, industrial or chemical plants, or even just crowded towns or cities, to name just a few.

We have looked briefly at individual power places earlier in this section, but there are also more general places where the energies are different, perhaps more pronounced, and can be perceived as either positive or negative. These are normally special places in nature that feel powerful, sometimes beautiful, sometimes foreboding. The geography of the land, and the rock and water beneath, can have a major effect of the energy felt in such places. Mapping these areas, either by feel or dowsing, has given us what are known as ley (or dragon) lines, and form part of a global grid of energetic connections. Sacred and culturally significant sites are often found on confluences of such ley lines, although little credence is given to this within the scientific community. And that is not a surprise as there are no scientifically proven instruments to measure such lines of energy. Perhaps one day there will be and the property prices near such hotspots will rocket.

Suffice it to say that there are a myriad of energies constantly bouncing around us, being absorbed and being radiated. It is clear that, with the right tools, they can all be measured but, as has been said before, science will always lag behind what actually is. Until there are instruments sensitive enough to detect all the energies of the Universe, the existence of some of the more subtle ones will always be in doubt. However for those that feel them, they will forever be real. Therefore trust you instinct and if you feel weird near an electrical pylon, a certain person or in a particular place, tune in to your senses and discern what the issue is. If this negative feeling is overly effecting you it is best to clear your energetic field, the energy of your home, and bring in some energetic protection.

You can clear your own energy field by using some of the previously described clearing and letting go exercises, and purge you home by smudging or burning incense, by beating a drum, chanting or singing, whilst holding onto the intention of clearing your space. Try to have a window or door open at either end of your home and go into every room, flushing the energies through, seeing the unwanted leave and replaced by fresh, uplifting and loving energy.

When it comes to protection I have always struggled with the necessity of such an action, as it is based in fear rather than love. Why should protection be needed? Shouldn't coming from a place of love be enough? Well yes I believe that is true, but I can guarantee that I have not always been able to get to that place of love, especially when I am out of sorts, feeling ill, have my attention distracted by real world issues, or am getting all my buttons pressed in a confrontational encounter. Coming from a place of love then becomes extremely challenging. This is why perhaps asking for and generating your own protection is prudent. It was once explained to me as having your own bouncer at the door, just in case of trouble. An insurance policy if you will.

Forms of protection vary, from calling in spirit, deities, holy people or totem animal allies, visualising protective auras, colours or bubbles around you, using an imagined shield or mirror to reflect back unwanted energy, or reciting prayers, spells or mantras for protection. Go with what feels right for you, but if protection and being protected are of paramount importance to you I suggest looking online for further information and techniques.

However, I believe that being in balance and in love, with yourself and the world, and sharing that love, is the best form of protection.

Authenticity

Most of this book is concerned with looking at life from different perspectives, taking a deep look at yourself and moving to a more connected and spiritual life, but ultimately you have to be you. Life is not about being someone else. So accepting your faults, your strengths, your mistakes and your shadowself, whilst looking to improve where you can, is all part of being your authentic self. Some authentic living tips from Lyn Christian, founder and coach at SoulSalt, are:

- Speak your opinions honestly in a healthy way.
- Make decisions that align with your values and beliefs.
- Pursue your passions.
- Listen to the inner voice guiding you forward.
- Allow yourself to be vulnerable and open-hearted.
- Set boundaries and walk away from toxic situations.[25]

Lyn goes on to say,

> *"When you discover how to be your authentic self, you live in the flow. Creativity and abundance come to you effortlessly. Consistently living up to your core values leads to self-confidence. You trust yourself, and know that you can overcome obstacles when pursuing your goals. When you learn how to be real, you also create genuine relationships. You express yourself honestly, and therefore, attract like-minded people who support you, for who you really are."*

---

[25] Lyn Christian, *How to Be Your Authentic Self: 7 Powerful Strategies to Be True*, 22/03/21, *SoulSalt.com*.

Neil Pasricha, author of *You are Awesome*[26], adds:

> *"When you're authentic, you end up following your heart, and you put yourself in places and situations and in conversations that you love and that you enjoy. You meet people that you like talking to. You go places you've dreamt about. And you end up following your heart and feeling very fulfilled."*

A considered life

The human condition and how to live well has been at the centre of human thinking for millennia. Perhaps the clearest guidelines came from the philosophies of the ancient Greeks, in particular, Socrates, Plato, Aristotle and the balanced and restrained approach to life as prescribed by the Stoics.

Stoicism still holds true even if one is on a path that includes spirituality or religion, although much philosophy shuns the need for any faith in a force or entity separate from the self. If you have doubts around some of the more esoteric or fuzzy areas of spirituality and religion then the more rational approach offered by stoicism and similar philosophies may fill any gaps.

Some pointers from the Stoics:

- *Turn life's obstacles into opportunities.* Embrace life's challenges as a way to advance and improve. There are lessons to be learnt from the issues that come our way, from the dramas and traumas, however unwanted they seem at the time. Look back at your *Life CV* for your own examples. (See *The South* section.)

---

[26] Neil Pasricha, You are Awesome, 2019, Gallery Books.

- *Focus on what you can change and don't worry about the things you can't.* Only your thoughts and actions are under your control, everything else is not. You always have control over how you respond to a situation or a problem. Waiting for spiritual intervention, the hand of God, or any other helping input, is deferring to that which you cannot control. It may well happen, you may be able to influence it but I suggest it is prudent not to wait, and to take action yourself. You have to take the reins of your own life, and, if at all possible, your death. (See *The West* section.) The Serenity prayer is stoic advice we are probably all familiar with:

> *God, grant me the serenity to accept the*
> *things I cannot change,*
> *Courage to change the things I can,*
> *And the wisdom to know the difference.*

- *It is not events that disturb people, it is their judgement about them.* When you are affected by a situation or encounter what is being reflected back to you? What are you seeing? And, more importantly, what are you not seeing or understanding?

- *We suffer more in imagination than in reality.* Don't dwell in the mind.

- *Don't fear death. Use it to give your life value.* We all die eventually so don't waste the precious time that you do have. Live immediately. *Carpe diem*, seize the day. Don't put off till tomorrow what you can do today. Take action.

- *Take time to review your day.* Practice having a daily reflection or a moment of peace for contemplation and meditation, and spend time in gratitude for what you have.

- *Maintain perspective and see the bigger picture.* Take the Eagle/Condor view. (See *The East* section.) Take a step back and realise that nothing is ever as important as it seems in the moment. Of course, bad things can and do happen, so don't be surprised by them, be prepared for them.

- *You never stop learning.* Keep an open mind and allow yourself the freedom to learn and improve. Spiritually we are children and know so little. Don't be ashamed to ask for help. (See *The North* section.) As Plato said, *"The more I know, the more I realize I know nothing."*

- Approach life with curiosity and assume that everyone you meet may know something you don't.

- *Test and stretch yourself.* Associate with those that will improve you. Welcome those that you can improve. Share the love.

The poem *If*, by Rudyard Kipling (1865-1936) written in 1895, is an example of Victorian-era stoic wisdom and restraint, and voted Britain's favourite poem in a 1995 BBC poll:

> *If you can keep your head when all about you*
> *Are losing theirs and blaming it on you,*
> *If you can trust yourself when all men doubt you,*
> *But make allowance for their doubting too;*
> *If you can wait and not be tired by waiting,*
> *Or being lied about, don't deal in lies,*
> *Or being hated, don't give way to hating,*
> *And yet don't look too good, nor talk too wise.*

If you can dream - and not make dreams your master;
* If you can think - and not make thoughts your aim;*
If you can meet with Triumph and Disaster
* And treat those two impostors just the same;*
If you can bear to hear the truth you've spoken
* Twisted by knaves to make a trap for fools,*
Or watch the things you gave your life to, broken,
* And stoop and build 'em up with worn-out tools.*

If you can make one heap of all your winnings
* And risk it on one turn of pitch-and-toss,*
And lose, and start again at your beginnings
* And never breathe a word about your loss;*
If you can force your heart and nerve and sinew
* To serve your turn long after they are gone,*
And so hold on when there is nothing in you
* Except the Will which says to them: 'Hold on!'*

If you can talk with crowds and keep your virtue,
* Or walk with Kings - nor lose the common touch,*
If neither foes nor loving friends can hurt you,
* If all men count with you, but none too much;*
If you can fill the unforgiving minute
* With sixty seconds' worth of distance run,*
Yours is the Earth and everything that's in it,
* And - which is more - you'll be a Man, my son!*

Love and fear

There are only two emotions at the root of all we do. We act out of love, or we act out of fear. Love is our natural state, but there is also a place for rational fear. It helps keep us safe from predators, hypothermia, dehydration, being burnt, falling from a height or other potentially dangerous situations. It triggers our fight or flight response, boosting our energy levels to be able to deal head on with the issue, or escape it, if that is deemed the best course of action. However our encounters with rational fear are very much limited in the modern world as rules, safety measures and cultural norms have restricted, reduced or even eliminated such threats.

Has this gone too far? Has the health and safety culture robbed us of feeling this rational fear, having this adrenaline pump through our veins, connecting us to the vibrancy and aliveness of the real world? Is this reflected in the uptake of extreme sports and escapist action packed video games, or the rise in popularity of horror movies and scary TV shows, providing the necessary shock our primal self calls for? Similarly, have we become so cosseted by the nanny state and mollycoddled as children by fearful parents that we have to look to irrational fears as a substitute? Do these irrational fears spread their tendrils far into our psyches, hijacking our imaginations, fuelled by sensationalist headlines in the media and online? Perhaps a more nature connected and considered life can diminish such irrational fears.

Write down an issue you have, or a question you want answered. Then write below what you are doing about it or the answer as you see it. Below this, clear your mind and write down the answer to the question, *what would love do?* What is stopping you following this path of love?

With any issue, to coin a phrase from an online course facilitator, "Love on it."

Epilogue

Going deeper with shamanic healing

The exercises and practices shared in this book have some linkage and similarities with contemporary shamanic healing work, but to understand more you will need to work directly with a practitioner or similarly experienced spiritual worker, either to further your learning or to work on yourself at a deeper level.

Contemporary shamanic practitioners hold their healing sessions in a sacred and safe manner, creating a space for the client to understand themselves at a deeper level and, in doing so, be able to understand any current negative issues, see their own true potential and release any blockages holding them back, whilst being fully supported and protected in the process.

The terminology for some of the healings and shamanic processes varies between practitioners and is often rather poetic, mystical and spiritual in language, with labels such as illuminations, soul retrieval, past life clearing, contract breaking, or entity extraction commonly used.

However, the important part of any shamanic healing is the clients willingness to work with and let go of any issues, traumas or painful experiences, illness, or negativity. It is this readiness to move forward and the intention that comes with it that holds the true power. If you are resistant to change, not wanting to be in the healing session, or in denial of any potential benefits, it is unlikely that you will be given any insight or feel an improvement, and will probably come away with an unfavourable view of the experience. It is therefore prudent to give a shamanic practitioner at least two, ideally three sessions so that you can become familiar with the process. As mentioned in the *exploring exercise* in *The East* section, when trying something new there may be wariness and insecurity on the first attempt, understanding on the second, and confidence there after. That said, if you have worked on yourself already then often one session is enough to make major breakthroughs.

In my work a healing session is about one and a half to two hours in duration and involves an initial consultation before the client is asked to lay on a therapy/massage couch whilst I conduct the contemporary shamanic work. I will use one or more of the objects from my spiritual altar, called a *mesa* (Spanish for table), which is the Q'ero term for a medicine bundle, or a portable table of sacred objects, each with a specific healing purpose. The treatment often includes the gentle laying on of hands, use of rattles, drum, voice or bells, and other shamanic tools to assist the process (some of which, including my mesa, are shown in the photo on the back cover of this book). During the process a variety of feelings, emotions or physical sensations can come up to be released, and it is always asked that the client be open to whatever happens, and allow it to unfold knowing that they are in a safe, protected and loving space. This is a very loose outline as the details will always depend upon the clients needs on the day.

Some sessions may be conducted outside, during a walk in a nature for example, where the connection to *Mother Earth* is palpable, or even held remotely, as energy and intention are not limited by location, as the science of quantum entanglement is now beginning to shed light upon. (See *Father Sky* section.)

A shamanic healing can bring about great emotional shifts, as sometimes years (or even lifetimes) of *baggage* are surrendered and transmuted, allowing the client to grow and move forward, feeling more in balance, more themselves, and can illuminate a clearer *soul path*. Personally I believe shamanic healing sessions are effective for many issues from physical ailments, emotional or mental imbalances, stress and anxiety, to personal development, spiritual connection and growth.

Shamanic healing is also just as powerful (sometimes more so) when working within a group environment, and the many forms this shared experience can take. Drumming circles, healing shares, seasonal celebrations, fire ceremonies, group healings, or specific courses or workshops all have their place, and offer chances for the individual to learn, heal and grow, whilst linking into ancestral celebrations, community togetherness and strengthening their connection to Great Mystery and *what is*.

Final thoughts

Shamanism, and the other spiritual areas explored, have really only been touched upon in these pages, but the connections and crossovers into other forms of spirituality and nature honouring are abundant in the modern world, as more and more people hear the call of *Mother Earth* and the life she supports.

All manner of books, workshops, online tutorials and courses are available so try and seek out authentic practices and teachings that resonate with you. Remember though you are the result of evolution, a long line of ancestors behind you, over a kilometre long. Some traditions and practices have stuck, some have been elaborated upon, some have even become sacrosanct. However, over so many generations some have also been distorted or lost, so sometimes you may need to create your own. Find what feels right for you, and trust your instincts.

It is my hope that within these pages you have found some tools and techniques to help you navigate your life path in a more authentic way, and understand a little more about contemporary shamanism and the relationship we all have to life on this planet.

In *The South* you worked with your past, finding lessons in the events that have occurred during your life, finding healing where it was needed. *The West* moved you into and through your fears, learning to accept death as a part of life and honouring any loved ones that have passed. *The North* asked you to engage with your senses, and connect with and nurture your inner child, so that you can be more open to the wonder that exists in everyday life whilst giving thanks to those that have been before. *The East* showed you that maybe there is a bigger picture you are not seeing, a calling based on your own abilities to take you closer to your dreams. *Mother Earth* helped you strengthen your connection to the natural world, to the elements and all life upon this planet. With *Father Sky* you looked heavenward, beyond the Earth, and embraced the infinite and unimaginable, realising that you are part of the web of life, even if much is not known to you. You have a right to be here. And as such, you stand in the middle of your world, in *The Centre*, from where you were asked to find your own balance, choosing how you wish to live in a truly authentic manner.

However small you may feel at times, when compared to the eight billion other people on Earth, the enormity of the planet, the scale of the solar system and mind boggling size of the known universe; a speck of dust on a grain of sand in an infinite sea; *you* are everything. You are king, queen, creator, destroyer. You are your own god or goddess, and all powerful in the kingdom of *you*. You can make a difference, not only to your own life but to the lives of others you share it with, be they human or animal. And for what purpose? Yes, to be the best you can, but also to share your gifts, your medicine, to help others and ultimately be of service in the survival and proliferation of life on this incredible, sacred jewel of a planet we call home.

Be part of the solution, not the problem. Be open to and drive change. Be the change the world needs. Look to where your deepest longing meets the planet's greatest need, or as Frederick Buechner puts it, "The place God calls you to is the place where your deep gladness and the world's deep hunger meet."

I'll leave you with the poem that I first came across in my twenties whilst travelling, that has provided inspiration and comfort in equal measure ever since, *Desiderata*.

With much love
Trevor

Spring 2022

Desiderata
(latin "things desired"), published in 1925.

Go placidly amid the noise and haste and remember what peace there may be in silence.

As far as possible, without surrender, be on good terms with all persons. Speak your truth quietly and clearly and listen to others, even the dull and ignorant; they too have their story.

Avoid loud and aggressive persons, they are a vexation to the spirit.

If you compare yourself to others, you may become vain and bitter; for always there will be greater and lesser persons than yourself.

Enjoy your achievements as well as your plans.

Keep interested in your own career, however humble; it is a real possession in the changing fortunes of time.

Exercise caution in your business affairs; for the world is full of trickery but let this not blind you to what virtue there is; many persons strive for high ideals, and everywhere life is full of heroism.

Be yourself.

Especially, do not feign affection.

Neither be cynical about love; for in the face of all aridity and disenchantment, it is perennial as the grass.

Take kindly the counsel of the years, gracefully surrendering the things of youth.

Nurture strength of spirit to shield you in sudden misfortune but do not distress yourself with imaginings. Many fears are born of fatigue and loneliness.

Beyond a wholesome discipline, be gentle with yourself.

You are a child of the Universe, no less than the trees and the stars; you have a right to be here, and whether or not it is clear to you, no doubt the Universe is unfolding as it should.

Therefore be at peace with God, whatever you conceive God to be, and whatever your labours and aspirations.

In the noisy confusion of life, keep peace with your soul.

With all its sham, drudgery and broken dreams, it is still a beautiful world.

Be careful.

Strive to be happy.

Max Ehrmann (1872-1945)

Acknowledgements

Thanks firstly must go to those that have gone before, and to all the indigenous peoples across the globe who keep alive the old ways and are willing to share their knowledge and wisdom, with a special thank you to the Q'eros of the Peruvian highlands.

Thank you to my teacher Skie Hummingbird for her guidance, support and humour over the many years, and to her husband Red and the numerous others met, shared with, and learnt from, within the Sungate family, whilst training, on a course, or just popping round for a cuppa. And talking of the odd cuppa, cheers Matt Keane for sharing so much, and always having the kettle on.

Thank you to the individuals, groups and societies that champion honouring the indigenous ways and mother nature, and who have helped me on my path, such as Nicholas Breeze Wood & Faith Nolton with their quarterly magazine Sacred Hoop, The Way of the Buzzard, The Sacred Trust, Embercombe, The Animas Valley Institute, and Peace Retreat to name just a few.

To all the shamanic practitioners, spiritual and energy workers out there trying to make a difference, I salute you.

Much gratitude goes to all the holders of drum circles, healing shares, and seasonal celebrations, especially to Jo Gray and Pete Wardle for their joy of drumming, endless enthusiasm, and for helping me birth my own hand drum many years ago.

For help with putting this book together a big thank you to Mark Dowding. And for the inspiration to go it alone, thank you Sue Stone. However self publishing (and self editing) my first book does mean all the mistakes, grammatical errors and poor English are on me. So my apologies for any you find.

Finally, a huge thank you to my friends and family, especially to mum in spirit, dad and Margaret, and Alison, Simon, Ruby and Anna, for all their love, support and understanding.

Printed in Great Britain
by Amazon

10020379R00162